SEEKING A BETTER URBAN FUTURE

IPS-Nathan Lectures

Print ISSN: 2630-4996
Online ISSN: 2630-5003

IPS-NATHAN LECTURES

SEEKING A BETTER URBAN FUTURE

CHEONG KOON HEAN

Published by

World Scientific Publishing Co. Pte. Ltd.

5 Toh Tuck Link, Singapore 596224

USA office: 27 Warren Street, Suite 401-402, Hackensack, NJ 07601

UK office: 57 Shelton Street, Covent Garden, London WC2H 9HE

British Library Cataloguing-in-Publication Data
A catalogue record for this book is available from the British Library.

IPS-Nathan Lecture Series — Vol. 5
SEEKING A BETTER URBAN FUTURE

Copyright © 2019 by Cheong Koon Hean

ISBN 978-981-3279-39-1
ISBN 978-981-3279-96-4 (pbk)

For any available supplementary material, please visit
https://www.worldscientific.com/worldscibooks/10.1142/11246#t=suppl

Desk Editor: Sandhya Venkatesh
Design and layout: Loo Chuan Ming

Printed in Singapore

THE S R NATHAN FELLOWSHIP FOR THE STUDY OF SINGAPORE
AND THE IPS-NATHAN LECTURE SERIES

The S R Nathan Fellowship for the Study of Singapore was established by the Institute of Policy Studies (IPS) in 2013 to support research on public policy and governance issues. With the generous contributions of individual and corporate donors, and a matching government grant, IPS raised around S$5.9 million to endow the Fellowship.

Each S R Nathan Fellow, appointed under the Fellowship, delivers a series of IPS-Nathan Lectures during his or her term. These public lectures aim to promote public understanding and discourse on issues of critical national interest.

The Fellowship is named after Singapore's sixth and longest-serving President, the late S R Nathan, in recognition of his lifetime of service to Singapore.

Other books in the IPS-Nathan Lecture series:

CONTENTS

FOREWORD

Singapore is an anomaly. It is a city-state; the city is the country and the country is the city. We have no sovereign hinterland. Everything that we need for a country has to be accommodated within our island, which is no larger than the metropolitan area of London. This is a unique situation that no other city in the world has to deal with. Nevertheless, thanks to great foresight and good planning by our predecessors, we have become one of the most liveable cities in Asia despite our limitations. After some five decades of independence, a whole generation has now grown up in a green garden city, with easy access to clean water, good facilities and decent housing. We have come to expect these comforts and a quality environment as the natural order of things.

But is it? Past success is no guarantee of future success.

What is the likely urban future of Singapore? Can we sustain our quality of life and even surpass where we are today?

I do not believe that anyone can give an answer with absolute certainty. We live in a complex and uncertain world. Singapore will face both external and internal challenges. We will have to contend with global trends, which all countries face. These include globalisation and rapid urbanisation, cyber connectivity, demographic challenges, climate change threats, and even terrorism. All these threaten the future of our cities. As highlighted by previous S R Nathan Fellows, there will be many 'unknown unknowns' that we cannot anticipate. We face the difficult task of planning for an uncertain future under VUCA conditions — where there is volatility, uncertainty, complexity and ambiguity.

However, what we can do is to try to prepare for the 'known unknowns'. Thinking through the issues that we need to address would help us to watch for and deal with different scenarios, shifting gears as necessary in the process.

Given our urban challenges, I have devoted this series of lectures to a discussion on cities and urban life, speaking as an architect-planner. Having been involved in the planning and development of Singapore for many years, my approach will naturally have a more physical orientation, with a focus on the development and management of cities. I speak as a practitioner who has to deal with the realities of life on a daily basis, and who has to work within the real world of limited resources. Planners are also jugglers, trying to find the right balance in meeting many needs and multiple interests. This forms the backdrop for what readers might find to be rather pragmatic and down-to-earth views.

The Three Urban Circles

The theme of my IPS-Nathan Lecture Series is 'Seeking a Better Urban Future'. The lectures cover three major topics wrapped around urban issues, ordered in descending scale from macro to local levels. We will start by examining inspiring cities at the global level, followed by an examination of Singapore's urban future at a national level, and finally exploring the future of heartland living at a more local level. These topics are interlinked, and I have illustrated them as three 'urban circles':

The first lecture, which is the outermost urban circle, will draw insights from the laureate cities of the Lee Kuan Yew World City Prize, a prize that is given out to an outstanding city every two years. As a founding member of the Prize and a nominating committee member since its inception, I have had the privilege and opportunity of analysing these cities closely to see what makes them tick. These cities hold many lessons for other cities and for us.

SEEKING A BETTER URBAN FUTURE

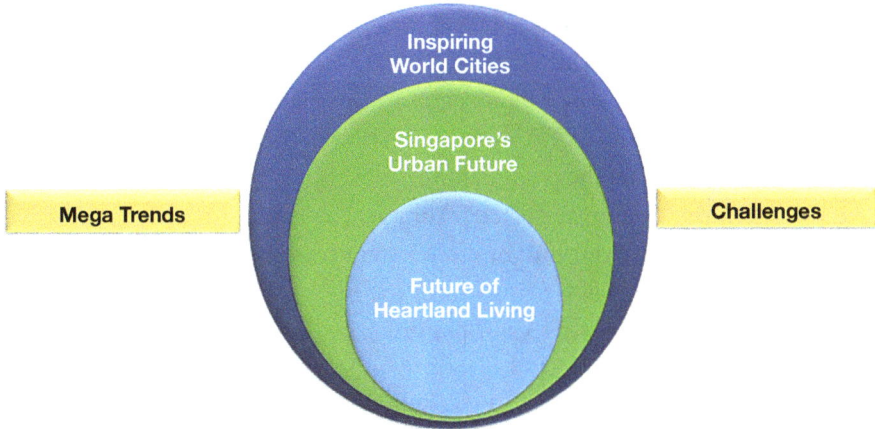

Singapore needs to pay attention to what is happening in cities around the world. As a small city-state, we make a living by being relevant to the world, given that we have no domestic market to speak of. This means that we have to compete with other cities and stay ahead, so that we can claim a place for ourselves in the international arena.

We must continuously learn from other cities. Mature cities, in particular, provide a mirror for us to reflect on where we might be headed in the coming decades so that we can anticipate issues ahead of time. Observing how they handle their challenges may provide us with some clues to the types of urban solutions that we can adopt.

Some cities are also a rich source of highly innovative ideas. This is why I make it a point to visit different cities regularly, to observe what others are doing and to learn from best practices. I often return with a sense of urgency, after I see the swift progress made in many of these cities. This gives us a push and spurs us to action. We cannot afford to be self-absorbed, inward-looking, or complacent. To stand out from the pack, we need to have an aspirational vision, supported by bold ideas and projects. It is critical to establish our branding and positioning internationally and to generate interest so as to draw businesses, investments and talents to our shores. At the same time, fresh and innovative initiatives will engender a sense of excitement, buzz and pride among our citizenry.

The second urban circle looks at Singapore on a national scale. Here, we start to identify potential trends that are looming on the horizon and discuss what these trends might mean for Singapore. There will be both threats and opportunities. How do we plan in an age of rapid change and uncertainty? What are the potential urban responses that can better prepare us for the future? There are very few solutions in the world that are directly applicable to us given our unique circumstances of having limited land and resources. We will have to think out of the box, adapt best practices from others by modifying them to suit our context, or develop completely new solutions for ourselves.

The third urban circle looks at Singapore's heartlands — our HDB Towns. Whilst we can carry out many intellectual discussions and debate on international and national issues, my experience is that the man in the street is most concerned about his immediate local environment. This affects his day-to-day living experience. Indeed, a 'man's house is his castle'. With more than 80 per cent of the population living in public housing, the quality of the living environment in our HDB heartlands establishes the concept of 'home' for the Singaporean like no other. We need to continually strive to improve the quality of our towns as we build new areas and redevelop others. But with a housing stock of almost a million existing flats, we will also need to keep upgrading our older towns to ensure a good living environment for these towns too.

For Our Future Generations

When I was first invited to accept the nomination as the 5th S R Nathan Fellow, I was initially reluctant as I thought there were many others more eminently suitable. After lengthy persuasion by Mr Janadas Devan, Director of the Institute of Policy Studies, I finally relented for two reasons.

First, President S R Nathan had always shown great interest in urban issues and in the development of the city during his tenure. He was often enthusiastic, supportive and encouraging when we shared with him new ideas and projects that were being developed. Delivering these lectures as a Fellow under his name is my small contribution to honour President Nathan's legacy.

Second, I hope that these lectures can spur productive and constructive conversations, and generate good ideas so that we can collectively meet the challenges ahead of us. More importantly, I do hope that more Singaporeans will:

a) have a greater awareness of what it takes to manage the complexities of a city;

b) understand the circumstances and challenges faced by Singapore, and take a holistic view of the choices and trade-offs; and

c) realise that developing a city requires collective action from government and multiple stakeholders — in particular, its citizens play a critical role in ensuring a city's economic success and building the deep emotional and social bonds that makes a city a home and country.

We are a small country, but we can have big and bold dreams. We have shown that we can create something out of very little. We need to carry this spirit of optimism forward and safeguard a better future for Singapore.

ABOUT THE MODERATORS

Mr Wong Mun Summ is a founding director of WOHA, an international award-winning architectural practice based in Singapore. He is Professor in Practice at the Department of Architecture, School of Design & Environment, National University of Singapore. He sits on the Nominating Committee of the Lee Kuan Yew World City Prize, and other design advisory panels in Singapore.

Professor Chan Heng Chee is Chairman of the Lee Kuan Yew Centre for Innovative Cities at the Singapore University of Technology and Design and Ambassador-at-Large at the Ministry of Foreign Affairs of Singapore. She is also Chairman of the National Arts Council, a member of the Presidential Council for Minority Rights, a member of the Constitutional Commission 2016, and Deputy Chairman of the Social Science Research Council.

Professor Lily Kong is Provost and Lee Kong Chian Chair Professor of Social Sciences at the Singapore Management University (SMU). Prior to joining SMU, she was a faculty member at the Department of Geography of the National University of Singapore, where she held various senior management roles. She is known internationally as a social-cultural and urban geographer who has studied urban social and cultural change in Asia over the last 30 years.

Lecture I

WHAT MAKES A CITY SUCCESSFUL?
LESSONS FROM INSPIRING CITIES

The Rise of Cities

J ohn F. Kennedy once said, 'We will neglect our cities to our peril, for in neglecting them we neglect the nation' (Kennedy, 1962). President Kennedy's words carry deep meaning where, today, more than half of the world's population live in cities. Going forward, the urban population will grow from four billion in 2015 to six billion by 2050, of which over two-thirds will be living in cities (United Nations, 2014, p. 217; World Bank, 2018).

The speed and scale in which cities are growing in order to accommodate the urban population have resulted in large urban agglomerations. Today, there are 28 mega cities, where each has more than 10 million inhabitants. By 2030, the number of mega-cities will increase to 41. Tokyo is projected to remain the world's largest city with 37 million inhabitants, followed by Delhi with 36 million (United Nations, 2014, p. 16). The cities around us in Africa and Asia will be some of the fastest-growing.

Rapid urbanisation brings about a whole set of urban challenges — there is accelerated but unmet demand for utilities, facilities and services, with many cities often in traffic gridlock and choked with pollution. Lack of affordable housing and income inequalities are also pressing needs to be addressed for the nearly one billion urban poor who live at the fringes of cities in informal settlements. In more mature cities, ageing infrastructure poses dangers and risks. The more developed economies are faced with policy conundrums arising from demographic challenges such as falling Total Fertility Rate, and ageing population and immigration. The increasingly volatile weather conditions brought on by the onset of climate change are also putting cities to the test. As cities consume close to two-thirds of the world's energy and account for more than 70 per cent of global greenhouse gas emissions (World Bank, 2018), it is critical that they are developed in a more sustainable and environmentally responsible manner.

On the other hand, cities are engines of growth, generating over 80 per cent of the world's GDP (World Bank, 2018). For instance, London accounts for almost half of Britain's GDP, while the Boston-New York-Washington corridor and greater Los Angeles account for about one-third of America's GDP (Khanna, 2016). Cities can also provide services and amenities to a population more efficiently in view of their compactness. Managed well, cities can be incubators for innovation, ideas and inventions, and can contribute to sustainable growth and high productivity.

The Lee Kuan Yew World City Prize: Inspiring Cities Around the World

Jamie Lerner, former Mayor of Curitiba, said, 'Cities are not the problems; they are the solutions' (Bilgrami, 2008). If cities are symbols of hope and development for humankind, we must find innovative solutions to help them overcome their challenges, and to secure a good quality of life for the millions living in them.

Singapore faces many similar challenges with other cities. However, on top of those usual issues, we operate under severe land and resource constraints. In addition, we are not only a city, but also a country. It is out of sheer necessity that we are strong advocates of sustainable development for the past 50 years. We have an interest in the development of urban solutions and in learning from successful cities from around the world.

Thus, in 2008, the Urban Redevelopment Authority (URA) and the Civil Service College set out to develop a unique prize, the Lee Kuan Yew World City Prize ('the Prize'), to seek out cities which are best in class, from which other cities can draw inspiration and ideas. The Prize would honour cities for their outstanding achievements and contributions to the creation of liveable, vibrant and sustainable urban communities around the world. It was officially launched in June 2009 at the Singapore International Water Week, which also confers the Lee Kuan Yew Water Prize.

I had the privilege of being involved in conceptualising the Prize with the dedicated Prize Secretariat team at the URA, and have served in the Nominating Committee of the Prize since its inception. When developing the Prize, we asked ourselves the key question, 'What are the attributes of successful cities from which the world and Singapore can learn?' There is no lack of plans being formulated by cities. Unfortunately, many of these plans are never implemented because cities are often hampered by a lack of direction, weak urban planning processes, lack of financial and regulatory mechanisms, and insufficient institutional capacity to realise their plans. There is also an inability to sustain implementation due to constant political changes and lack of political will. Hence, when conceptualising the Prize, we put together a set of criteria through which we subject cities to close scrutiny. Through these lenses, we hoped to draw out the critical factors that make cities work.

City applicants have to be nominated for the Prize by a credible third party. The cities also have to submit the following details to make a strong case for themselves:

a. **Leadership and governance** information about the city. This would provide a good understanding of the city leader's role in the city's transformation, and the governance structure in place to drive the implementation of the city's plans.

b. **Key urban and policy solutions** that were adopted and implemented, leading to the city's transformation, and the extent to which these were innovative solutions.

c. **The impact, durability and sustainability of the urban transformations** from adopting the initiatives.

d. **The replicability and scalability of the urban and policy solutions** for other cities.

e. **Integration with the National / Regional / Metropolitan Level plan.** Cities exist within a larger context, relying on funding and major infrastructure to be provided at the federal and state levels. Close coordination at these levels becomes critical for the successful implementation of city initiatives.

In its assessment of the cities, the Nominating Committee also considers the level of effort put in and the impact of the improvements made relative to resources available, given their current level of economic development. We also seek out cities that are highly innovative in overcoming their complex challenges. Detailed data has to be submitted to substantiate the improvements claimed, such as improvements in employment and environmental quality, and reduction in traffic congestion over a sustained period of time. The Nominating Committee then submits its recommendations on the cities to be recognised to a Prize Council, comprising eminent persons for endorsement.[1]

Today, the Lee Kuan Yew World City Prize is a biennial international award currently into its fifth award cycle. In the past decade, we have received nearly 170 submissions covering six continents.[2] The Prize has been conferred on five outstanding cities: Bilbao (2010), New York City (2012), Suzhou (2014), Medellín (2016), and the latest, Seoul (2018). Though only one Laureate city is conferred the Prize during each award cycle, cities that have made vast sustained improvements to the lives of their citizens could receive a 'Special Mention'. In some cases, the cities needed more time for their efforts to bear fruit. One case in point is Medellín, which was a 'Special Mention' city in 2014, but emerged as the Prize Laureate City in 2016.

---

[1] As of August 2018, the Nominating Committee is chaired by myself, and its members are Professor Wulf Daseking, Mr Lim Eng Hwee, Dr Chris Luebkeman, Professor Marilyn Taylor and Mr Wong Mun Summ. The Prize Council is chaired by Mr Peter Ho, and its members are Mr Flemming Borreskov, Ambassador Chan Heng Chee, Ms Helen Clark, Mr Park Won-Soon and Mr Ilmar Reepalu.
[2] Submissions were received from cities in Africa, Asia Pacific, Europe, Middle East, and North and South America.

LEE KUAN YEW WORLD CITY PRIZE

CYCLE	LAUREATE	SPECIAL MENTIONS				
2010	Bilbao	Melbourne	Curitiba	Delhi		
2012	New York City	Ahmedabad	Khayelitsha	Brisbane	Copenhagen and Malmö	Vancouver
2014	Suzhou	Yokohama	Medellín			
2016	Medellín	Auckland	Sydney	Toronto	Vienna	
2018	Seoul	Hamburg	Kazan	Surabaya	Tokyo	

Table 1: The Lee Kuan Yew World City Prize Laureates and Special Mentions (2010 – 2018) (Source: Urban Redevelopment Authority)

The Prize has accumulated successful, exemplary demonstration projects with each award cycle, thereby building up a body of knowledge to provide useful lessons and new benchmarks for cities around the world. Although it is a 'young' prize, it has grown in stature as many cities, including many top global cities, compete to be recognised by the Prize.

Tales From Different Cities

Each of the winning cities tells an inspiring story. Many of the Laureate and Special Mention cities share important underlying traits that have led to their success. In this lecture, I will focus on the Laureate cities to draw out what some of these key traits are. Many of these traits run through almost all the Laureate and Special Mention cities, though to different degrees.

I am mindful that each city varies in scale and population size, in the level of economic development; each has a distinct historical, cultural and political context. For example, New York is a highly developed mega city with global reach. Bilbao and Suzhou are transition cities with a strong history and a developing economy, whilst Medellín is a developing city working to build up basic infrastructure and amenities for its people. They each adopt different approaches to best suit their specific contexts. Nonetheless, it is useful to examine and distil some best practices from these cities so that other city governments could consider whether they are useful for their particular situation. I have extracted some of these best practices below.

Lessons From the Prize Laureate Cities

(a) Plan long term and plan for implementation

The Prize Laureate Cities and Special Mentions have generally shifted away from the traditional blueprint master plan towards a longer-term, strategic-planning approach. This focuses on the process of decision-making. It is generally forward-looking and long-range, consisting of broad frameworks and spatial ideas. Being strategic means focusing on selected aspects that are important to overall plan objectives. Usually, the general planning goals are about sustainable development and spatial quality. Policy guidance at a city level is linked to national and regional plans. However, the strategic plan provides guidance for the development of detailed urban projects to ensure that the vision and planning goals are realised. So whilst cities seed the beginnings of a bold vision with a long-term comprehensive plan, these are backed up with robust detail implementation plans to realise the vision.

The process of formulating the plan is almost as important as the plan itself. Many stakeholders are brought on board to encourage an alignment of understanding among them. At the same time, these cities are mindful that the plan must be institutionally embedded to give a higher assurance of continuity and cooperation over different terms of political leadership.

Bilbao: From post-industrial decline to a city of culture and innovation
A good example that illustrates this approach is the Spanish city of Bilbao. It was a port city that gradually saw the decline of its industries along the river. A crisis point was reached when it was hit by devastating floods in 1983. To turn the city around, the city administration prepared the Bilbao General Plan (1989), which set out to reorganise and modernise its major industries and economic structure as its mining, steel and ship building

industries had declined in the 1970s to the 1980s. Successive leaders have continued to support and contribute to the implementation of this plan.

The highly valuable land along the river was recovered to enable the industrial economic activities to be restructured towards a knowledge-based and digital economy. Although it only had a population of about 430,000 at its peak, Bilbao positioned itself as 'the downtown' that serves the entire Basque Country, hence effectively extending its influence to reach a larger population of two to three million within a 300 km radius. Bilbao then drew up comprehensive plans to systematically execute 25 projects over 25 years, covering environmental improvements to the river, improving its airport and transport infrastructure, and injecting design, art and cultural projects to rebrand itself. These projects made the city far more attractive to investors, and transformed the city from a dilapidated industrial city into a knowledge-based economy. This demonstrated that successful urban development and

BILBAO – 25 PROJECTS OVER 25 YEARS

- Rehabilitation of the historical centre
- Enlargement of the port
- Freeing up the port and industrial space along the water
- Setting up Bilbao Ria 2000 (1992)
- The clean-up of the river
- Renovation and innovation along the river
- Old and new bridges connecting both banks of the river
- Bilbao's underground metro system
- Sondika Airport
- The Guggenheim Museum (1997)
- Further expansion of museums or art institutions
- Abandoibarra

- Transformations in the Ensanche area
- Relocating the Abando railway underground
- New tramway
- New public infrastructure
- New hotels
- Zamudio Technology Park
- Environmental improvements in neighbourhoods
- Bilbao La Vieja
- Conservation of built heritage
- Injecting new architecture
- Injecting art into the city
- Achieving international recognition
- Future projects (Zorrozaurre, high speed trains, knowledge institutions, creative economy)

Figure 2: Bilbao's 25 projects over 25 years
(Source: Municipality of Bilbao)

Figure 3: The renewed historical centre of Bilbao
(Source: Municipality of Bilbao)

regeneration require the integration of strategic vision with the systematic implementation of key infrastructure and urban projects at various levels.

Beyond just paper plans, a new institutional arrangement was set up to ensure that the plans get executed. The formation of Bilbao Ría 2000 has been a key instrument for Bilbao's transformation. Established in 1992 by Mayor Iñaki Azkuna as its founding Chairman at an initial investment of €1.8 million, Bilbao Ría 2000 oversees the recovery of brownfield sites (Bilbao International, 2000). It is also responsible for developing and re-integrating the sites into the fabric of the city to stimulate new urban and economic development. The partners of Bilbao Ría 2000, which included the Housing

Ministry, Bilbao Port Authority, railway companies and the Bilbao City Council, also allocated land to the company for concerted redevelopment. Bilbao Ría 2000 coordinated the land preparation, transfer of developmental rights, infrastructure provision, and land sales. As a non-profit company, it reinvested the financial gains obtained in recovered areas or strategic urban initiatives — such as the relocation of the port and the river clean-up, which enabled the entire rejuvenation effort to take off.

(b) Harnessing the power of partnerships and engagement to ensure implementation

Most of the winning cities clearly realised that their plans must also build social capital within their governance structures. Hence, many adopted participatory processes and engaged the community of stakeholders because it multiplies the effectiveness and impact of a policy or programme. The new plans tend to be more bottom-up, to enable a broader range of groups and civil society to give voice to their needs and aspirations. The plans then take into consideration the needs of various groups and achieve greater alignment with and among them. This process enhances the chances of successful implementation over a sustained period and across different political administrations.

Increasingly, public-private partnerships are also adopted as many cities lack resources or skills to build public infrastructure. Particularly in the developed cities, private sector investments are tapped to redevelop urban brownfield sites. The profit-oriented aims of the developer are then aligned with the aims of the cities to modernise and upgrade their infrastructure, regenerate physically, and restructure the economy.

New York: Successful reinvention and rejuvenation

New York is a particularly strong example of how a city has successfully tapped on the resource and enterprise of its private sector and stakeholders. It had gone through a period of decline from the 1970s to the 1980s due to disintegration and rising crime levels. With more people moving to the suburbs, the population shrank by 800,000 people for the first time. The 1990s marked the first signs of turnaround when then Mayor Rudy Giuliani

(1994–2001) managed to make the city safer and improve education and social services.

Mayor Michael Bloomberg, who came on board in 2002, worked swiftly to prevent a further slide in the city. He focused on improving infrastructure, reclaiming abandoned industrial sites for redevelopment, renovating and creating new parks and public spaces, and spearheading economic opportunities and developments. By partnering community organisations, he formulated PlaNYC and delivered on many tangible outcomes.

'PlaNYC: A Greener Greater New York' is the city's first consolidated, comprehensive plan consisting of 127 initiatives, addressing land, water, transportation, energy, air and climate change issues and preparing New York City for a more sustainable future. It was released in 2007 and updated in 2011 with 132 initiatives, in anticipation of one million more residents by 2030. The plan came about after an extensive public consultation exercise to align city agencies, community leaders, interest groups, businesses, and the general public towards achieving common goals. In a visit to New York some 10 years ago when PlaNYC was being formulated, I came away impressed that much of the consultation efforts were driven ground-up by many young volunteers. The young lady who briefed me said that because PlaNYC was the result of broad-based inputs from many stakeholders, it was likely to last beyond Mayor Bloomberg's administration. This was probably a deliberate strategy to ensure the longevity of the ideas in PlaNYC!

The Mayor's Office of Long-Term Planning and Sustainability (OLTPS), which is charged with the development and implementation of PlaNYC, was institutionalised in 2006. A local law, enacted in 2008, calls for PlaNYC to be updated and revised every four years, and to plan 20 years ahead following each review. OLTPS also reports on 30 sustainability indicators and tracks the impact of the initiatives systematically. This is then released in yearly progress reports, providing accountability to the citizens, and ensuring the city is on target for 2030.

An example of how the private sector injected innovation into New York City is the highly successful High Line project. The project actually started out as a citizen-led initiative ('Friends of the High Line') by two young men who wanted to save an old elevated railway line from demolition. The idea received the support of Mayor Bloomberg and the railway line was saved and repurposed. The High Line was subsequently developed as a significant injection of much-needed public space and relief to counterbalance the high density of New York City. Capitalising on the High Line, city authorities grasped the opportunity to catalyse the rejuvenation of the districts adjacent to it. Part of the urban design intention was to keep the scale of buildings next to the High Line lower. By allowing developers to transfer their development rights to sites in another designated area, sites adjacent to the High Line could still realise their development potential. This spurred the development of a slew of residential, commercial and hotel projects designed by well-known architects along the High Line. The investment of US$160 million of public and private funds has led to private investments of almost US$2 billion. Such is the power of a citizen-led urban innovation, combined with a supportive and market savvy city administration, which then catalysed an entire area.

Mayor Bloomberg's strong business acumen led the city to forge strong partnerships with non-profit organisations and private developers to come up with practical financing mechanisms to sustain and maintain assets. To ensure that they are sustained after implementation, projects such as the High Line, Brooklyn Bridge Park, and New York City Plaza Program are maintained with funding from not-for-profit organisations such as Friends of the High Line, Brooklyn Bridge Park Corporation, and Business Improvement

Figure 4: New York City's High Line
(Source: New York City Department of Parks and Recreation)

Figure 5: Brooklyn Bridge Park before (left) and after its project implementation (right) (Source: New York City Department of Parks and Recreation)

Districts (BIDs).[3] BIDs are allowed to issue bonds for capital improvements. The city also grants private sector partners the right to sub-concession on city property in exchange for maintenance responsibility. Private sponsorships, revenues collected on-site and abutting business properties make up annual revenues to ensure the partners' ability to maintain assets in the long run.

Seoul: Visionary leadership and active citizen engagement

Seoul is another example of a dramatic transformation from top-down planning to ground-up collaboration with the community and stakeholders. Prior to the 1990s, the planning for Korean cities was carried out by the national government in a top-down process. After the 1990s, city leaders were given greater autonomy in urban development. But they faced increasing resistance from people who felt left out of development decisions in the past. Faced with rapid population growth, a burgeoning car population and environmental degradation, successive visionary leaders elected in the 2000s took a completely different tack to reverse the previous top-down management structure when dealing with the city's many urban challenges. City leaders realised the need to solicit input and buy-in from both citizen and stakeholders through rigorous engagement.

---

[3] A BID is a business-led and business-funded body formed to improve a defined precinct area. It is a formal place management model, such as Times Square Alliance in the United States and Better Bankside in the United Kingdom. BIDs are operated independently by the private sector to complement various services provided by the government, such as improvements in areas of security, transportation and maintenance.

Since 2009, the right to approve the master plan was transferred to the Mayor. The formulation of the 2030 Seoul Master Plan is seen as a turning point in the city's planning process. It is the first master plan to be legalised by the Mayor, and is required to be updated every five years. Under the leadership of Mayor Park Won-soon, the city made participatory planning its primary focus; citizen participation became the norm for all plans and bottom-up processes. The planning process became a citizen-led process facilitated by top-level commitment, as can be seen from the preparation of the 2030 Seoul Plan.

To implement difficult urban development projects, the city carried out rigorous engagements and negotiations with conflicting parties representing various interests. These parties included groups concerned with issues like traffic disturbances, business losses and heritage restoration. The city even formulated a set of conflict management strategies and deployed a dedicated team of trained negotiators within the Seoul Metropolitan Government to help the city win over even the most reluctant people, and to seek a resolution and way forward. Such a participatory approach has enabled the implementation of a series of catalytic projects, which involved the painful decision of removing roads from the city.

For example, the Cheonggyecheon project involved the removal of an elevated highway so as to restore a former stream and provide a much-needed new public space for the city. The Cheonggyecheon project became the catalyst that sparked the redevelopment of many buildings on either side of the stream. The entire area has now been rejuvenated.

Figure 6: The Cheonggyecheon Stream in the 1970s (left), and where there was an elevated highway in the 2000s (right)
(Source: Seoul Metropolitan Government)

Figure 7: Restoration of Cheonggyecheon stream, Seoul
(Source: Seoul Metropolitan Government)

Figure 8: Seoullo 7017, a conversion of the Seoul Station Overpass into
a one-kilometre long lushly planted elevated walkway
(Source: Seoul Metropolitan Government)

To further empower citizens, the Public Participatory Budget System allowed citizens to decide on the use of up to 5 per cent of the city budget (or 55.5 million KRW). For greater accountability, the City Ordinance requires the monitoring of the outcomes of the Master Plan on a yearly basis where results are publicised to provide opportunities for feedback. Mayor Park is clearly the key driving force behind the philosophy of citizen participation, which has percolated throughout the city.

(c) Focus on the fundamentals of improving quality of life, ensuring greater inclusiveness and reducing inequities

Ultimately, cities are built for the people who live there. According to Harvard Professor Alan Altshuler, 'In order to achieve prosperity, every city must provide incentive for investment, hard work and entrepreneurship. While a degree of inequality is inevitable, extreme inequality devastates the lives of those at the bottom, leading to ill effects on health, crime, lack of community spirit and could threaten social instability'.[4] For many of the winning cities, the starting point was a recognition of the need to tackle deep-rooted issues in their social fabric, such as lowering crime rates, putting in place programmes to build a more inclusive city, and providing more equal opportunities for all. Improving the quality of life is high on their agenda.

Medellín: From impoverished city to a city of new aspirations
Medellín, the second largest city of Colombia, tells the compelling story of a city which has transformed itself from a notoriously violent city (it was once known as the 'murder capital of the world') to one that is being held up as a model of urban innovation within a span of two decades, despite the lack of resources when compared with richer cities. Over a sustained period, a succession of leaders have demonstrated the willingness to recognise and take on deep-rooted problems — the wealth distribution, lack of equity and opportunities, high crime rate, and lack of proper housing and access to basic

---

[4] This is based on an interview with Alan Altshuler, titled 'Planning and Innovation for City Success', and published in the World Cities Summit (June 2008) issue of Ethos. Alan Altshuler is the Ruth and Frank Stanton Professor of Urban Policy and Planning at Harvard University and is a former visiting Professor of the Lee Kuan Yew School of Public Policy.

Figure 9: Medellín
(Source: Urban Redevelopment Authority)

infrastructure such as water, sanitation and transportation. By providing greater accessibility to public transport, jobs, education and public spaces, Medellín's leaders have helped to reduce inequality and crime.

Despite limited resources, Medellín successfully took a pedagogical approach to merge social and spatial planning. A Strategic Plan of Medellín and the Metropolitan Area 2015 was conceived in the 1980s and 1990s to set the direction towards active citizenship. Urban interventions and the construction of buildings, roads, parks and public spaces became synonymous with social equity. The Land Use Plan of Medellín (POT-Plan de Ordenamiento Territorial), introduced in 1999 and last revised in 2014, became the roadmap that will define the city's development until 2027. Strategic Intervention Areas were identified where actions will be implemented to overcome deficiencies caused by urban imbalances.

Geographically, Medellín is a landlocked city that lies in Colombia's Aburrá Valley, which runs between two mountain ranges at the northern end of the Andes. Over the decades, many migrants set up homes on the slopes of these mountains, which became economically and socially isolated from other parts of the city. The uncontrolled spread of these *barrios*, or urban neighbourhoods, led to multiple problems, such as landslides that killed many inhabitants, and high crime due to the lack of opportunities and spaces for education and recreation. To alleviate this isolation, Medellín built the world's first cable car mass transport system (Metrocable), which ferries some 38,000 passengers daily between the hills and the city for less than a dollar a ride. The city also took former shopping mall escalators and installed these units in hillside neighbourhoods to make it easier for residents, especially the elderly and children, to get around. Taking this further, a new Ayacucho tramline using old tramcars retrofitted with pneumatic wheels was introduced in 2015. The cable car and tram systems, which are being expanded, offer vital connections to the existing Metro railway network that traverses Medellín's metropolitan area.

To address the environmental and social risks of informal settlements in the mountains fringing the city, Medellín created what is known as the

Figure 10: The Circumvent Garden, Medellín
(Source: Municipality of Medellín)

Figure 11: Public spaces at Santo Domingo, Medellín
(Source: Municipality of Medellín)

Circumvent Garden, a montane green belt that puts a halt to urban sprawl, but also provides public spaces and economic opportunities for the surrounding inhabitants. Apart from preserving the forests, Circumvent Garden prevents erosion and contributes to the city's pleasant climate. The Circumvent Garden also offers sports facilities and farming sites, and reduces the isolation of the hilltop communities. Furthermore, the city also took the unusual step of assessing and legalising most of the informal housing units that were structurally sound, rather than evicting illegal settlers on state land at the urban-rural fringe, so as to improve the social standing of these settlers.

In another part of the city called Moravia, there was a waste dump occupied by thousands of families. Medellín transformed the barren landfill into Moravia Gardens, a botanical 'garden of life' managed by members of the community. Medellín is also working to rejuvenate the areas fronting Medellín River.

Medellín found that the key to effective governance was through social innovation. It strives to empower its citizens by giving them a stake in the city and building trust and confidence. For instance, Proantioquia, a non-profit organisation of private businesses in the Antioquia region, actively serves as a platform for government and private companies to work together. They formulate policies and execute initiatives based on the principles of social responsibility and fairness. The city introduced UVAs (Unidades de Vida Articulada, or Life Articulated Units), which are essentially neighbourhood-level urban interventions that open up new public spaces, encourage citizens to interact with each other, and provide forums for sports, culture, and recreation. Medellín has a 'City for Life' motto that translates into equitable public space design. The UVAs around the city take different physical forms. For example, the city worked with Empresas Públicas de Medellín (EPM, a public utility company) to redesign water tanks as community facilities, with involvement from the community as part of the Life Articulated Units programme. Library parks also double as social nodes.

To help families break out of the poverty cycle, the Good Start Programme invests in the educational development of the youngest segment of society. To achieve this, the city has spent US$1.5 billion over the past three terms of government to build more schools. Medellín has also established a 'University + Company + Government' programme that creates an environment to encourage innovation among the youth.

To grow the economy, the city is now facilitating the development of a new technological district called Medellínnovation District. The 172-hectare district aims to transform Medellín's northern region through science, technology and innovation, with a mix of housing and economic activities to generate more than 28,000 jobs by 2023.

These initiatives, which focus on providing equal opportunities and social inclusion over the years, have generated positive outcomes. The city of 3.7 million inhabitants has reduced its homicide rates by 92.1 per cent since 1991, from about 368 homicides per 100,000 inhabitants to 28.9 per 100,000 inhabitants in 2015. Unemployment rates have been cut from 23 per cent in 1990 to 10.2 per cent in 2014. Extreme poverty fell from 19.4 per cent in 1991 to 2.8 per cent in 2015.

Medellín's brand of urbanism serves as a beacon for many developing cities. They took a finite amount of money and made improvements for the maximum number of people. They moved from building buildings to providing access.

(d) Multi-dimensional catalysts for change

Beyond strategic, two-dimensional land-use planning and infrastructure considerations, the successful cities brought in multi-dimensional catalysts to achieve high environmental spatial quality and programming to enrich the city's attractiveness. Culture, heritage, good urban design, place-making and programming are deployed innovatively and in combination, to enhance identity, vibrancy and city pride. These elements are also used to differentiate themselves, giving each city a unique character.

Bilbao: Culture and design-led transformation

Bilbao has had exceptional success in the use of culture and design to regenerate the city. Its strategy was to bring in international arts and culture to effect a symbolic transformation of the city and departure from its industrial past. High standards of design were sought in the execution of urban projects

Figure 12: Guggenheim Museum, Bilbao
(Source: Municipality of Bilbao)

Figure 13: 'Fosterito' subway entrance (left) and subway station (right) by Norman Foster in Bilbao

using world-renowned designers. One of the first projects commissioned was the development of the Guggenheim Museum by Frank Gehry, which opened in 1997. It became a key tourist attraction and spawned a series of tourism and hospitality-related industries. This 'culture driven' strategy became so successful that, internationally, it earned the moniker 'Guggenheim Effect'. (It should, however, be noted that the Nominating Committee of the Prize took pains to explain that there were many other key factors underlying the success of Bilbao's transformation beyond the 'Guggenheim Effect').

Another key strategy was to use design to drive the physical improvements to the city. Almost every aspect of Bilbao city was subject to design consideration, and in particular, its public infrastructure. Visitors are welcomed at the magnificent Bilbao Airport designed by Santiago Calatrava. Norman Foster was commissioned to create the signature glass entrances to its metro network, which became affectionately nicknamed 'Fosteritos'. Collectively, these elements gave Bilbao a unique character, charm and branding.

Seoul: Dongadaemun's rejuvenation and Makercity Sewoon

Seoul, too, has used culture and design to good effect in transforming the city. It regenerated the declining manufacturing sector in Dongdaemun by

Figure 14: Dongdaemun area regeneration with Dongdaemun Design Plaza, Seoul (Source: Seoul Metropolitan Government)

Figure 15: Makercity Sewoon, Seoul
(Source: Seoul Metropolitan Government)

Figure 16: Yonsei-ro Transit Mall, Seoul
(Source: Urban Redevelopment Authority)

redeveloping it as a hub for culture, fashion and design. A key catalyst was the Dongdaemun Design Plaza designed by Zaha Hadid, that opened in 2014. It is a cultural hub for art, design and technology, linked by a plaza to a landscaped park, providing a much-needed green oasis in the city.

Good design is not necessarily about new, expensive, large and iconic building interventions. It can also be used to good effect to improve the day-to-day urban infrastructure used by citizens to enhance liveability, safety and the aesthetics of the city. For example, innovative design can be applied to the repurposing of existing buildings. The Makercity Sewoon project in Seoul links seven commercial superblocks that were built in the 1970s, through the sensitive insertion of a new linear space to incubate projects run by young entrepreneurs alongside the original occupants. This simple urban intervention stitches together disparate parts of the city through improved pedestrian connectivity, and enhances the vitality of an old area by introducing new uses and more young people. The Mapo Culture Depot is a conversion of disused oil tanks into a cultural venue and public space, offering new perspectives on repurposing infrastructure while preserving collective memories of the people.

Suzhou: Preserving heritage and tradition
Suzhou is a shining example of how heritage and tradition have been preserved in the midst of rapid city growth. It has undergone a remarkable

Figure 17: Skyline of Jinji Lake CBD, Suzhou
(Source: Department of Publicity, Suzhou Industrial Park)

Figure 18: Pingjiang Historic District, Suzhou
(Source: Pingjiang Historic District Preservation & Restoration Co. Ltd.)

transformation in just two decades. Suzhou had initially benefitted from Singapore's experience and contributions in the 1990s when it set up its first industrial estate. Singapore had helped to prepare a master plan for its industrial township and city centre. However, it has since independently put in place many initiatives that have propelled the city forward. The Suzhou City Master Plan was drawn up in 2003 to achieve growth by increasing the city's liveability while maintaining strong business vibrancy and cultural heritage. The Master Plan comprised several key plans, the land-use city plan, industrial development plan, the eco-environment consideration plan, a water protection plan, and a heritage preservation and restoration plan.

Suzhou has stood out as 'a city that recognised the importance of cultural conservation even as the drive for modernisation gained momentum' (URA, 2014). To preserve Suzhou's Old City comprising its historical and cultural core, Suzhou redirected urban growth pressure to a new Jinji Lake Central Business District, a mixed-use centre built for the 21st century.

A heritage preservation and restoration plan was put in place not only to systematically preserve the Old City, but also to revitalise the growth of the community living within it. Apart from outlining the historic districts, zones and traditional areas, the plan also sets out guidelines for strengthened preservation of the cultural heritage, relics, historic architecture, waterways and landscapes of Suzhou, e.g., Pingjiang Historic District Feature Protection and Environment Restoration Plan, and the Pingjiang Road and Streetscape Protection and Restoration Plan. Suzhou has also restored eco-sites, such as the Stone Lake Scenic District. By leveraging on its 2,500-year-old historical legacy, Suzhou has created a strong sense of place that translates to a city that is rich in both tradition and modernity.

In addition to cultural sensitivity, I would like to mention that we were pleasantly surprised to find out that Suzhou had adopted inclusive policies towards its migrant workers who came from other Chinese cities. As Suzhou's economy took off over the past two decades, it received many migrants seeking employment. Unlike other Chinese cities, where provisions for migrant workers are highly restricted through the *hukou* system, Suzhou took a more inclusive approach. It implemented a residence permit, covering the non-native population, and incorporated housing of non-native urban residents into housing security at the institutional level, where they could enjoy similar housing funds to the native residents. The construction of social housing saw a significant increase from 30,000 units in 2008 to 110,000 in 2012.

Suzhou has also established a guideline on public school enrolment, to simplify procedures, and ensure justice on equal footing and equal treatment of students without discrimination. Children of non-native residents who have lived in Suzhou for over one year, with relatively stable housing and income, can have access to public school and compulsory education by law, similar to their native peers.

Public spaces, parks and place-making

The winning cities recognise that well designed and well maintained public spaces and parks promote people's health and well-being, relieve a city's high-density environment, help build a sense of attachment to the city, and foster stronger community bonds. New York has spent more than US$3.8 billion to renovate and create new parks since 2002, and another 600 park projects are in the pipeline. By 2030, New York would have upgraded and acquired 1,900 hectares of parkland and public space throughout the five boroughs, with the goal of allowing every New Yorker to live within 10 minutes' walk of a park.

Beyond just the design of physical spaces, 'place-making' is applied whereby activities are programmed to take place in these spaces, often led by the community, so as to activate these spaces and promote community interaction. A successful example of active place-making is Bryant Park, a popular park that has multiple programmes throughout the year, including New York's Fashion Week. Other cities such as Seoul and Bilbao similarly have an active calendar of events throughout the year, held in great public spaces.

(e) Building environmental resilience and adopting sustainable practices

Climate change poses new challenges. The winning cities have actively worked towards sustainability goals to reduce their carbon footprint and address the effects of climate change and natural disasters.

New York: PlaNYC's green goals

In New York, PlaNYC initiatives aim to cumulatively contribute towards the goals of reducing greenhouse gas emissions by 30 per cent below 2005 levels, by 2030. These initiatives include a cycling network to encourage cycling, better building energy management systems, improved transit commutes and MillionTrees NYC.[5] The city has adopted new research and design strategies to achieve greater resilience against environmental and man-made risks. In total, US$920 million has been allocated to six projects in New York, New Jersey and Long island, to enable the construction and integration of key infrastructure elements to protect coastal neighbourhoods. Innovative proposals for flood protection include the use of marshlands, berms, a network of slow streams, breakwaters and tidal flats.

---

[5] MillionTrees NYC is a public-private programme that aims to plant one million new trees across New York City (NYC)'s five boroughs over the next decade, so that NYC can increase its urban forest.

(f) Strong leadership and good governance to lead and drive change

Benjamin Barber, author of *If Mayors Ruled the World*, views mayors as pragmatists, whose job is to get things done. (Barber, 2013). As the 'homies' who are elected to lead in their own communities, mayors have the ability to lead, take action and mobilise the masses. In the Laureate cities and Special Mentions, the mayors have played key roles. They provide foresight, proactively built up institutions, and put in place good governance processes, regulatory structures and financing mechanisms that ensure the continuity of the formulated plans beyond their administrations. They often champion and set in motion strong private-public partnership models to finance and sustain development projects. They are passionate about their cause, building up a dedicated team around them, and are usually in office for a sufficient period of time to see through many of their initiatives.

For instance, Mayor Iñaki Azkuna, who was Mayor of Bilbao for more than 10 years, was the key driver of Bilbao's transformation, supported by a committed team of officials. He established Bilbao Ría 2000 as a platform to align government, business and community towards a shared vision for Bilbao, and became Bilbao Ría 2000's founding Chairman to drive his vision for Bilbao.

Mayor Michael Bloomberg, who came on board in 2002 and served two terms till 2013, was instrumental in pushing multiple initiatives that brought great improvements to New York and generated economic opportunities and new developments. He did much of this by mustering citizenry, businesses and stakeholder involvement. He strengthened New York City's administrative structure by bringing in highly capable and dedicated commissioners for key city departments such as Transportation, Planning, and Parks & Recreation.

Mayor Park Won-soon of Seoul is totally committed to participatory planning and utilised this engagement mode to drive through many difficult urban initiatives to transform Seoul. He is extremely hands-on. When I called on him in his office, he had a whole wall of LCD screens behind his desk that monitor all aspects of the city's functions.

Similarly, Medellín had a number of mayors who worked consecutively in transforming the city. The individual widely regarded as laying the foundations for Medellín's development is Sergio Fajardo, who was Mayor of Medellín from 2004 to 2007 (Eveland, 2014). In later years, Mayor Aníbal Gaviria Correa of Medellín, who served from 2012 to 2015, had been a charismatic leader who inspired the city to overcome its limitations through non-conventional and creative urban solutions. He created a participative society with strong public-private-people cooperation and improved social and living conditions to bring about greater equity in granting access to urban utilities and facilities for even the poorest communities. His good work is now continued by the current Mayor Federico Gutiérrez who was elected in 2016.

Recognising that mayors play a critical role in the development of cities, the World Cities Summit, which was established by the Centre for Liveable Cities and the URA, incorporates the biennial Mayor's Forum as an important anchor of its programme. This Forum brings together mayors from more than 100 cities across the world to discuss urban issues, share experiences, and resolve new challenges together.

Success Factors and a Continuous 'Work-In-Progress'

As can be seen from this study, the development of cities is a complex process that is technical, political and artistic all at the same time. It is often about balancing interests for a shared future, and requires strong leadership and engagement to work out the resources to be shared, what citizens value, and the kind of legacy to leave for future generations. It is also about building institutional capacity and frameworks to ensure plans and programmes can be implemented over different political administrations.

In my view, a compelling vision and a comprehensive long-term view are pre-requisites for the successful development of cities. However, to attain the long-term goals, detailed plans have to be worked out and embedded within an institutionalised process to secure a higher chance of getting the plans implemented over different terms of government. The principle is not about developing a 'planned' city in the traditional blueprint mode, where plans often become outdated very quickly in an era of dynamic changes. Rather, it is about a 'city that plans continually', at times taking the necessary sharp turns in response to changing situations, but always having the long-term vision and end goal in mind.

In a world of increasing complexity with multiple voices and limited resources, cities can no longer do it all by themselves. Hence, whilst the top-down approach provides the institutional structure and framework to guide city plans, more participation and involvement needs to be harnessed from stakeholders, citizens and public-private-people partnerships to implement and sustain transformation through co-creation. This also builds the social resilience necessary to face the threats of risks, disruptions and crises.

To secure ground support and greater societal stability, city strategies need to prioritise the fundamentals of improvement in the quality of life — by ensuring public safety, promoting inclusiveness, and creating a more equal society for its people. Layered onto this is the adoption of highly innovative ideas to catalyse development. A combination of strategies wrapped around culture, heritage, good design, place-making and programming add depth to the city's image and brand, and differentiate them from others. These catalysts help to create distinctiveness, define identity and social memories, and instil greater pride in the city for its people. In addition, the cities are mindful of the need to secure greater resilience and sustainability to mitigate potential climate change threats.

A critical success factor is the emergence of strong and often charismatic leaders in these cities. These leaders create the moments of opportunity and vision that push the city on a trajectory of transformation. But no leader can deliver plans on their own. They need to build up a team of dedicated and capable people who provide the ideas and technical capability to deliver on the plans.

Whilst many of the winning and Special Mention cities have done very well relative to cities around the world, there is really no perfect city, and every city is a 'work-in-progress'. Each city has to continue to work to address its challenges.

Providing affordable housing continues to be one of the biggest challenges. For example, New York has yet to fully find ways to scale up the provision of affordable housing to cater for the planned population growth of an additional one million people by 2030. Medellín still has large segments of the population living in informal housing. Much of Bilbao's resources have recently been channelled into ambitious new projects that require high investments and maintenance, while it currently has no active measures to provide affordable housing.

Upgrading and developing new infrastructure will continue to be a challenge. Like many other developed mega cities, New York faces the challenge of renewing ageing infrastructure, be it bridges or metro lines. In the case of Medellín, despite the development of its public transport network, more will need to be done to encourage people to switch from private to public transport so as to reduce traffic congestion. Suzhou would need to ramp up its rail network to provide a transit-oriented public transport system.

There is also a danger that cities, particularly emerging cities in Asia, pursue 'iconic' projects as an end in themselves without sufficient sensitivity to the existing city fabric. Quality and elegant architecture, good aesthetic sense, and urban design that enhance the city and human experience will still need to be consciously pursued.

Reflections on Singapore

Although each city recognised by the Prize continues to be a 'work-in-progress', they have indeed provided useful lessons of what it takes to be a successful city. Singapore's experience mirrored much of what these winning cities have gone through. Our developmental success story from slum to modern metropolis stems very much from strong leadership with good foresight. Our leaders and decision-makers took a long-term planning perspective, and built institutional capacity and strong governance processes to ensure that our plans are well conceived and implemented. From the day we became an independent nation, we recognised the importance of ensuring social equity and greater inclusiveness. We have worked to reduce inequities largely through governmental transfers in subsidised housing, education and health. Despite our resource limitations, we strive to develop in a sustainable manner, and put in high priority the goal to be a liveable city.

Going forward, there are some major trends looming that will pose significant risks, challenges and disruptions to cities. On the other hand, there are opportunities to develop creative urban solutions for our unique circumstances. In my second lecture, I will explore what these trends are likely to be. In particular, we will delve deeper into what these trends mean for Singapore, and explore the potential urban responses that can better prepare us for the future.

References

Altshuler, A. (2008, June). Planning and innovation for city success. *Ethos.*

Barber, B. (2013). Why mayors should rule the world. TED Global. Retrieved from https://www.ted.com/talks/benjamin_barber_why_mayors_should_rule_the_world

Bilbao International. (2000, December 17). Bilbao Ría 2000. Retrieved from http://www.bilbaointernational.com/en/i/

Bilgrami, Z. (2008, June 6). Maverick mayor: 'Eco-architecture not ego-architecture!' CNN. Retrieved from http://edition.cnn.com/2008/TECH/06/06/jaime.lerner/index.html

Eveland, J. (2014, September). Medellín transformed: From murder capital to model city. Lee Kuan Yew World City Prize. Retrieved from https://www.leekuanyewworldcityprize.com.sg/media/feature-articles/medellin-transformed

Kennedy, J. F. (1962, January 30). John F. Kennedy: Special Message to the Congress Transmitting Reorganization Plan 1 of 1962. The American Presidency Project. Retrieved from http://www.presidency.ucsb.edu/ws/?pid=8699

Khanna, P. (2016, April 13). How much economic growth comes from our cities? World Economic Forum. Retrieved from http://www.weforum.org/agenda/2016/04/how-much-economic-growth-comes-from-our-cities

United Nations. (2014). *World urbanization prospects: The 2014 revision.* New York: United Nations Population Division of the Department of Economic and Social Affairs.

Urban Redevelopment Authority Singapore. (2014). 2014 Prize Laureate: Suzhou. Retrieved from https://www.leekuanyewworldcityprize.com.sg/laureates/laureates/2014/suzhou

World Bank. (2018, June 22). Overview: Urban development. Retrieved from www.worldbank.org/en/topic/urbandevelopment/overview

Question-and-Answer Session
Moderated by Mr Wong Mun Summ

Wong Mun Summ (WMS): Thank you, Koon Hean, for bringing us round the world in 60 minutes. I am on the Lee Kuan Yew World City Prize's nominating committee and it is indeed very interesting to see the nominated cities and to compare them with others.

I want to kick-start this Q&A by asking you to comment on Singapore in light of two lessons you mentioned. One, on harnessing the power of partnership and engagement to ensure implementation of plans: does Singapore fare well in this regard? The other lesson that I was hoping you could comment on is building environmental resilience and adopting sustainable practices. I am particularly interested in these two because I think that, for the other lessons, it is clear that we have done very well.

Dr Cheong Koon Hean (CKH): That is the subject of my second lecture. But I will touch on it a little bit. On the power of partnership and engagement, I would say that we went through a process over time in our approach to planning. I spent some time at URA in my career, and I could see the changes. I must say that, in the early days — maybe two decades ago, maybe slightly more — planning tended to be more top-down. At that time, a lot of people did not quite understand what urban planning was. So sometimes cities have to go through a certain phase. By the time we did the Concept Plan in 1991, we knew that we needed to do a lot more engagement, and I remember organising many public consultations. We had town hall meetings and people were invited to comment on the plans. As time went on, the engagement became more frequent; some of you may have participated in them.

In HDB, we are doing the same. We engage the public a lot, and so does the URA. If you look at many of the agencies such as PUB, they are all doing a lot of public-private partnerships. But we must also understand that engagement is actually a complicated process, because you must understand who you are engaging, and you must understand whether they understand what you are engaging them on. I will not go into the details, but engagement is quite an art, to distil useful things and feelings and inputs from people. For different types of groups, you engage using different modes, to get the best inputs you can.

The second question is on building resilience and sustainability. I absolutely agree that it is very important. I would say that we are very mindful of this now. Perhaps the world suddenly is very mindful because of climate change; the world was not very mindful of this several decades ago. Singapore also has in place a sustainability blueprint, which brings together many of the efforts to put in place sustainability initiatives.

As an island-city state, there are a lot of threats. For island states with a lot of water around them, sea-level rise is one of the most important issues to think about. We have already started to conduct many studies on how to mitigate this threat. Actually, I am going to cover this in my second lecture, so if you are interested, please come.

WMS: Actually that was what I was going to ask for my next question. *The Economist* refers to Singapore as the only fully functioning city-state. Being a city-state with limited land, we do not have a hinterland. Is this an advantage or a disadvantage?

CKH: Well, life does not come in a nice package. We had always been aware of land and resource constraints. You cannot run away from it. The Chinese have a saying, 'You cannot choose the family you are born into.' You are here in Singapore, and you have to recognise the constraints.

On the other hand, city-states generally move very fast. Decisions can be made faster because they tend to have a single-tiered government. You are also far more integrated in your decision-making. So you are nimbler, and you can make decisions. Well, if you ask, 'Is it an advantage or a disadvantage?' Singapore has had all these constraints, but where are we today? Not bad, I think, given all these constraints. The key is, how do we sustain that success into the future? How do we think about it? Because as we build up, you do face many challenges.

Participant: I am from Taipei, Taiwan, but I have lived in Singapore for a long time, and I love this city. I grew up here, and it is a good place to be. But I cannot help but think of waste management, which I was hoping that you would talk about. Every time I am in Seoul and Tokyo, I am impressed by how big the city is and how well managed their waste is. The back lanes are always very clean. I cringe every time my friends come to Singapore — they say, 'Singapore is so clean!' and I keep thinking, 'Well… you have not seen some parts.'

So, when you give your lecture on the HDB heartlands, I hope you talk about things like our toilets. Taiwan has just gone for a no-plastic ban, and Singapore is really not very clean. I do not know what you have learnt from the other cities, like Seoul, on how they manage waste. And what is it that they do with their communities that do not deploy more cleaners, but actually get people to move a certain way and help themselves?

WMS: So it is about waste management, and how Singapore could be better.

CKH: I fully share your view. I did not give an example of one city that is quite amazing, and that is Yokohama. Yokohama is a Special Mention city; they did not win, because the competition is actually quite stiff. But they are an excellent city. When I went to Yokohama, the thing that impressed me most is their waste management. Do you know how many types of waste every household sorts? Make a guess. Seven? Good number. Anymore? Twenty plus? Well, okay, that is quite a lot. The answer is 15! And we cannot even get people in HDB flats to put recyclables in one chute and organic waste in another.

So when you ask me, why people cannot do that, I also ask the same question. It is not a government problem; it is about the ethos of society.

I watched a fantastic documentary about how people in Taiwan deal with trash. Every day or every week, the truck comes around, it plays music or rings a bell which sounds like an ice-cream truck. And everybody brings down the trash. There is no chute for you to open and throw, there are not even bins that you could probably throw trash into, downstairs. They bring their own trash down to the rubbish truck. And it became a social gathering place, because everybody is bringing down their rubbish.

Now, then my question falls back to you, which is, how do we achieve that as a society? In fact, my second lecture talks a little bit about that. It is not about, 'Can the government do something about it', but 'How can *we* do something about it'? The government can facilitate, but we need to work together. So, if you have great suggestions, you should post them.

Yokohama is amazing; the Japanese are very disciplined. But it is partly the nature of their culture. If someone does not bring down the trash in time for the truck to collect and does not sort it out, the neighbours will all look at you. It is a little bit of a shaming method that they use. The rubbish truck will also not collect their rubbish. But here I cannot do that, because people drop their trash into the common chute and I do not know who has dropped the rubbish in — it is a practical issue. But you are right. I wish we could do more and I suppose mustering community is very important in this. We are all in it together.

Participant: One of the challenges you might have come across would be in Medellín. You mentioned that they built the Circumvent Garden to prevent urbanisation from growing more into the hilly areas. But then, what do you think about how global cities are facing more and more in-migration? How do cities tackle that? Because then when you talk about citizen participation, how do you involve these citizens that have just moved into the city?

There are also ethical challenges as to whether you can displace people. Can you resettle them, and do you have spaces to resettle them? What are your priorities? So for example, Cheonggyecheon, the one example you gave from Seoul, was it simply that there were no property owners around that area? Then it would have taken on a different challenge because then you have to bring them on table. How do you discuss their property rights, resettle them, where else do you place them, and will they agree to it? So what do you think about in-migration and the growing population of cities?

CKH: As I do not have time to address all your questions, I will answer very broadly. I do not think there is one solution for every city. So for example, with in-migration, housing is one big issue. Medellín just recognised the informal settlements — as long as they are not crumbling down and killing someone, they allow it. In South America, because there are not a lot of resources, for example in Curitiba, they will do a 'site-and-services' approach, which means all the government does is to bring in water and electricity, and then they let people build their own homes. The people can afford to build one room at a time using say, mudbricks, and they build a house over time. That is one solution. Another solution in big cities is to use the private sector to set aside, say, 20 per cent of affordable housing. Unfortunately, they cannot scale that up to cater to demand.

I do not have one answer because it is a very big issue for most cities and tied to that is in-migration. I did not mention this because there was not enough time — that I was very impressed with Suzhou. In China, they restrict the number of people coming to the city precisely for this problem that you talked about, where the city just keeps growing. You have the certificate, the *hukou* system. Without the certificate, you cannot live in the city. In Suzhou, they managed to give people who work in the city the right to education and housing. They added in a lot more affordable housing. So there is no one answer for every city as it depends on the resources they have.

WMS: I have another question from the spillover room. 'Singapore is the only global metropolis located on the equator. Outdoors here are hot and humid. Have you come across ideas on tackling our hot outdoor environment?'

CKH: When Mr Lee was alive, he used to say, 'Can you bring the temperature down and put a big dome over Singapore?' I am still waiting for the solution.

I think, in theory, what you should do in Singapore is to have more dehumidifiers, to remove moisture from the air. Actually, we are not that hot. It is 'sticky' because of the humidity, and there are many other cities hotter than us. Can you imagine, if you remove some of the humidity from the air, first, you will feel cooler and, second, you can collect the water and reuse it. That is a good idea, right? The problem is how to scale up, because all this takes a lot of energy.

There are ways to plan, to try to reduce the temperature a little bit, and make use of the airflows in the city. That is my short answer. There is technology to help you plan better — not that the technology reduces the temperature, but by helping you to plan better, you can actually channel winds and breezes in a certain way.

WMS: I think Singapore actually has done well through the greenery, and it is a lot cooler.

CKH: My National Parks Board (NParks) colleagues will tell you that the greenery can bring the temperature down by a few degrees. The urban-heat-island effect takes place as we keep losing trees and adding concrete and hard paving, so it gets a lot warmer. But there are ways to plan and reduce the urban-heat-island effect.

Participant: You have the privilege of knowing many cities. I want to ask, how can we distil all this knowledge into new master-planned cities? Because a lot of countries always want to build the next Brasilia, Putrajaya, Xiong'an, and you have done Tianjin Eco-City. How can all this be distilled so that when you do the next new city — a master-planned one — you have got the best and know it will work?

CKH: That is a very good question. I have people coming to me, asking, can we distil the best of Singapore and then write it into a formula, then apply it? Actually, you cannot. What I would like to say is, first, there is no perfect city. Second, there is no perfect formula, because every city is different. What I mentioned in the lecture is not a formula. The lessons from these cities are best practices. But you have to select carefully the appropriate practices for your city. A solution for New York may not be the right solution for Medellín.

So you need to be discerning. Cities do not become successful because of the masterplan. And as I have outlined in my lecture, it takes a whole ecosystem, good leaders, institutions and good governance. You need a great plan, but you also need all these things that make it happen, thinking, how do I finance some of these things? So, it is not so easy but you can, minimally from the spatial point of view, think about the good practices.

You really need the whole ecosystem and the governance structure. When I did the Tianjin Eco-City masterplan, it was not easy, because there were many people with many different ideas. And after you have done the plan, you can have changing administrations, and the plans keep changing. There are many cities that cannot keep to the plan. And I am not saying that 'you must keep to the plan' because that would fix the plan; it is too inflexible. But at least, when you change the plan, it is a rolling plan. You have to remember some of the original intentions, objectives and vision.

A lot of people come and tell me, 'Why do you even plan? Things are so complex. No need to plan, just react as you go along.' I do not subscribe to that, and I will explain why in my second lecture. In the case of Singapore, we are a city-state. We have limited land and we had better plan, because we cannot afford to make many mistakes.

So, there are no simple answers. But there are certain spatial principles that we all know — that you have to plan for a growing population, housing, good infrastructure, and a balance of recreation and greenery. These are very basic things that all planners and architects know they must do. But I am talking about considerations beyond that. How do you get things going? That depends a lot on decision-makers, the government and politicians to drive the plan.

Participant: You gave five best practices that we could take away or learn from cities, and among them, you mentioned how we must plan inclusively, providing the example of Medellín. But prior to that, you gave the example of New York and the High Line. As a tourist, I have been to New York and the High Line. It really is very impressive, but there is always the consideration of what it means for the community. I quote one of the co-founders of the High Line, Robert Hammond, who said that, 'We were from the community. We wanted to do it for the neighbourhood. But ultimately, we failed.' Because, at the end of the day, what happened in the Chelsea District is that the housing prices went up a lot.

CKH: It got gentrified.

Participant: Precisely. So my question to you is, you listed these five best practices, but how often are cities able to balance them? And if they cannot balance them, can we truly consider them to be successful?

CKH: It is difficult. That is one of the problems every city faces — gentrification. The Meatpacking District started great but it has become expensive now. So it is inevitable when people repurpose buildings. The creative class goes to a place because it is cheap. So when gentrification happens, you have a problem.

There are cities that try to ring-fence the problem. Start-ups are a good example — they operate in 'the backyard'. Some cities do set aside certain spaces with cheaper rental where you encourage start-ups. But inevitably, there is the economic side of it to consider.

It is like conservation. Do you keep buildings exactly the way they are? But conservation needs to consider the economic side of things too. If you cannot let the owner get economic value out of conservation, he has no money to restore the building. Who is going to pay for it? So it is a very fine balance. I have been asked this question many times, 'Why do you not bring back the old trades?' My point is, will the old trades survive in this world? How many of you will continue to buy the old wooden clogs, for instance?

So you have to strike a balance. For the High Line, the public can use it. It is a public space. It depends on the definition of 'for the community', and 'gentrification'. The developments on either side of the High Line pay taxes so that the government can provide parks and public spaces. And if you go to the High Line today, it is free. Nobody charges you for it. Are the New Yorkers better off? Yes, because they now have a public space in the middle of New York.

There are choices you have to make; trade-offs. There is no perfect world. And you have to make those choices. Most governments do both — you let the economy make the money, but with the money, you then do the transfers. In our case, there are transfers. You give to education, health, housing — that is how governments work.

WMS: I have another question here from the spillover room. You used Medellín as a case study. Could you comment more about the informality of the city, and if Singapore can learn from its 'non-planning'?

CKH: They had a plan! That is the whole point — they do have a plan. I think the question is about the planned versus the unplanned. So let me share with you my thoughts on that. You go down to Times Square, and it looks pretty chaotic, right? Do you think it is unplanned? All those billboards that you see? It is planned! They have rules this thick for the use of Times Square — the size of the billboards, how the billboard is going to be done. All these are planned, because they want to achieve a certain vision and vibrancy. And their regulations are thicker than the ones we have here, I assure you.

This is called 'planned chaos'. So may I also address another misunderstanding about the planned versus the unplanned? There are some things that need to be planned. These are the macro things when you deal with the city, such as the infrastructure, the broad land-uses, because you have to juxtapose a lot of these and you have to make sure that these are available for the city. These cannot be left unplanned — where you put the airport, the port. For the macro level, you have to plan.

But as you come down to the more micro and local level, this is where you can give a lot more say to the community, because it is right at their backyard. They can tell you what they like and what they do not like. But it cannot be a case of it being totally unplanned. How are you going to put a road through? How are you going to put an MRT line through if you do not plan decades ahead of time?

So when we talk about 'planned' and 'unplanned', we have to understand the scale we are talking about. It is the same for engagement. Certain types of engagements are actually very complex — you need a more professional type of understanding to be able to give a considered view. Other times, it is very easy. Everybody can give a view. But for the very complex issues, you need to be able to solve the technical aspects. And you have to plan for it.

Participant: In your experience, referring to these cities as well as to Singapore's experience, have there been instructive lessons from planning mistakes — things that we planned in good faith but did not turn out the way we thought, but were productive because we learnt something about how the city works or it created a new opportunity for us to improve?

CKH: I would say that, for most of the cities, the shortcoming tends to be the lack of affordable housing. It is a very difficult problem to solve. Usually they lack funding. Similarly, sometimes, the lack of infrastructure is a weakness. They have to find a way to do it. My own personal belief is that in many cities, there is a lot of angst among young people because of the lack of affordable housing.

For Singapore — we learnt along the way. I think what we can do better in is participatory planning. But do not get me wrong, participatory planning does not mean that you just go out and ask everybody what they want. It also means that you have to persuade people. It is not one-way, where people tell you, 'I want these one thousand things', and you have to say yes. It does not mean that, because it is not possible. There are so many interest groups and there are so many voices; you cannot satisfy everybody.

The thing we can learn from Seoul is that they have very good people who are able to discuss, negotiate and persuade. We lack that skill, and it is something we can learn. We are starting to do a lot of consultation, and persuasion is a skill. One of the challenges faced by most cities is the NIMBY ['Not in My Back Yard'] attitude, especially in the more developed cities, where income levels are higher and people are more educated. How do you have a good constructive conversation where you get people to understand that sometimes, it is for the greater good? Like better waste management? Now those are the skillsets we are still honing. We are not terribly good at it, but we are learning.

WMS: All good things must come to an end, so Koon Hean, I give you maybe the last word to say, to promote your next lecture. What are the disturbing mega-trends? Just a few, so we can look forward to your next lecture.

CKH: Well, for every challenge, there is always an opportunity. All cities are going to face demographic changes. Climate change and technology disruptions — these will be some of the types of challenges that we will face. And of course, for Singapore, we are completely open to the world. The economy is another concern, especially nowadays where there is a lot of discussion about world trade, and we depend on the world to make a living.

The question is how do we plan a city to try to deal with some of these challenges? That will be covered in my next talk.

Lecture II

ANTICIPATING OUR URBAN FUTURE: TRENDS, THREATS AND TRANSFORMATION

Introduction

A few years ago, I was invited to speak at an International Planning Congress in Sydney. I was pleasantly surprised when the host introduced Singapore as 'The Rock Star City', and quipped that this is because Singapore is a 'very well planned city'. What an accolade for Singapore, given that just five decades ago we were a city of slums and squatters. We have indeed come some way.

Singapore, at just 720 square kilometres, is about half the size of metropolitan London, and has a population of some 5.79 million people. We are land and resource constrained. Yet, in addition to the day-to-day facilities to support economic and social needs, we have to provide for major infrastructure requirements that enable us to function as a sovereign country. It is hard to believe that, on this little island, we house five airports, 17 reservoirs, several nature reserves, extensive land for military training, and one of the largest container ports in the world. Unlike London or New York, we have to provide for all these uses within our city. Despite our limitations, we have managed our urban growth reasonably well over the decades. For example, in 2017, Mercer ranked Singapore as the most liveable city in Asia (Mercer, 2017).

SINGAPORE VS LONDON

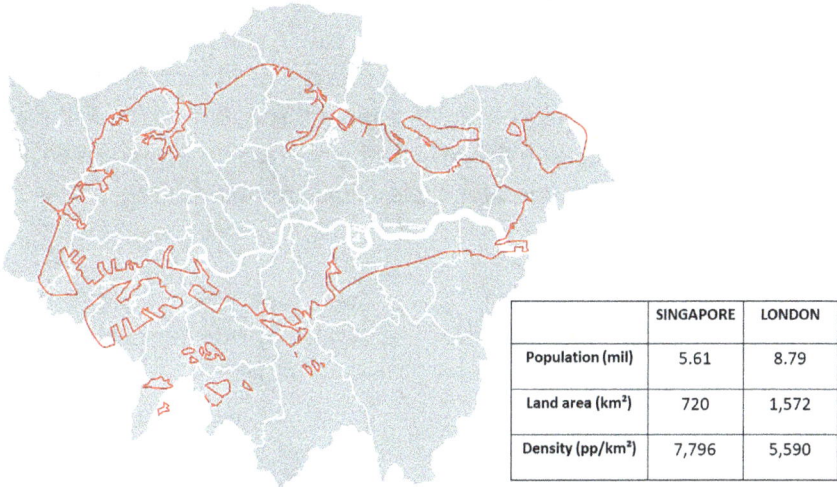

	SINGAPORE	LONDON
Population (mil)	5.61	8.79
Land area (km²)	720	1,572
Density (pp/km²)	7,796	5,590

Figure 1: Singapore (red outline) in relation to metropolitan London[1]
(Source: Housing & Development Board)

However, going forward, many changes — both external and internal — will pose challenges for us. What are these challenges, and how well are we anticipating them, so as to build an attractive urban future with a good quality of life?

Challenges

Maintaining economic growth and competitiveness

Singapore has enjoyed sustained economic growth since independence. Incomes have risen, and resident unemployment rate has remained low by world standards, at around 3 per cent. Nevertheless, as highlighted in the report by the Committee on the Future Economy last year, subdued global growth, rising anti-globalisation sentiments, and protectionist economics will hurt a small and open economy like Singapore's (Committee on the Future Economy, 2017). Remaining relevant and competitive, and tapping

[1] Unless otherwise credited, all figures, photos and tables are from the author.

on new opportunities for growth is imperative for us. Hygiene factors like good governance and stability, availability of skills, and a safe and friendly business environment continue to be important. As for physical aspects, we have to ensure that we remain an attractive and competitive city for businesses — with adequate space, reliable utilities and infrastructure, state-of-the-art connectivity (physical and virtual) and high liveability. This will enable Singapore to attract investments and talent, and grow business opportunities.

Mitigating Climate Change

The earth's climate is likely to change dramatically over the next century. Increased occurrences of extreme weather events, desertification and rising sea levels all directly threaten the world's cities. Fifteen of the world's largest cities are located in coastal zones vulnerable to sea-level rise and storm surges.

Singapore is not exempt from climate change. According to Singapore's Second National Climate Change Study, there has been a general uptrend in annual average rainfall from 2,192 millimetres in 1980 to 2,727 millimetres in 2014. Based on Phase 1 of the study, the long-term effects of climate change would lead to a temperature increase of 1.4°C to 4.6°C and a rise in sea levels of up to about one metre by the end of this century (National Climate Change Secretariat, 2018).

Sea level rise poses the most immediate threat. Much of Singapore lies only 15 metres above mean sea level, with about 30 per cent of our island being less than 5 metres above the mean sea level. Periods of drought can affect the reliability of our water supply, while sudden episodes of intense rainfall could overwhelm our drainage system and lead to flash floods.

A mean temperature increase of 1.5°C to 2.5°C could affect the natural diversity of Singapore's plants and put animals at risk, as this will alter our ecosystem's natural processes, such as soil formation, nutrient storage and pollution absorption.

Warmer temperatures mean that more vector-borne diseases like dengue could become endemic and more people would suffer from heat stress. Urban areas will become warmer as natural land cover gives way to buildings and other infrastructure that retain or produce heat. This induces the 'urban heat island effect'. Increased use of air-conditioning will also lead to higher energy demand and carbon emission.

The effects of climate change such as intense storms, floods or prolonged droughts will also threaten global food security. Singapore is particularly vulnerable to fluctuations in global food supply and prices as we import more than 90 per cent of our food.

Even as we continue to urbanise, we need to protect our city from the effects of climate change.

Preparing for an Ageing Population

Singapore faces the twin demographic trends of declining birth rates and an ageing population. Our Total Fertility Rate (TFR) has been below replacement level since 1977. TFR in 1976 was 2.1, dropping to 1.8 in 1977, staying below replacement level ever since. By 2030, one in four Singaporeans, or about 900,000 people, will be aged 65 and above, double the current number. The citizen old-age support ratio[2] will fall from 6.4 in 2010 to a projected 2.4 in 2030, based on the current fertility rate if there is no introduction of new citizens (Strategy Group et al., 2017). There has been much discussion on whether these demographic trends will affect Singapore's economic and social vibrancy, and how the impact could be partially mitigated by the longevity dividends accruing from a more productive senior workforce and new 'silver hair' industries (Institute of Policy Studies, 2017).

What is certain is that, as our population ages, we need to enable the elderly to remain physically healthy, economically active, and engaged with the community so that they can stay independent for as long as possible. Our physical environment needs to be designed for a more elderly society, with sufficient supporting facilities for them.

Managing Technology Disruptions

We are in the midst of a technological revolution that is changing how we live, work and relate to one another. There are many scientific breakthroughs and new technologies being generated. I will highlight a few that will have a more direct impact on how cities are planned, developed and managed.

---

[2] The old-age support ratio 'relates to the number of people who are capable of providing economic support to the number of older people who may be dependent on others' support' (Singapore Department of Statistics).

PREPARING FOR AN AGEING POPULATION: SINGAPORE IS GETTING OLDER

1990

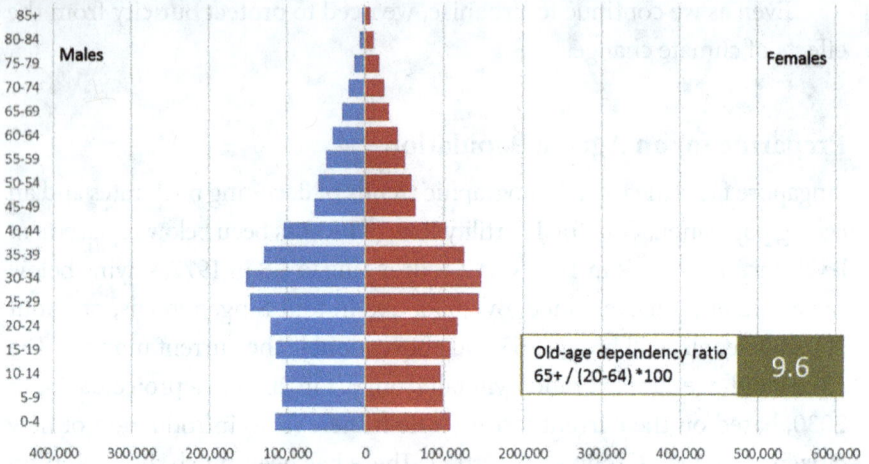

Males	Females

Old-age dependency ratio
65+ / (20-64) *100   **9.6**

2010

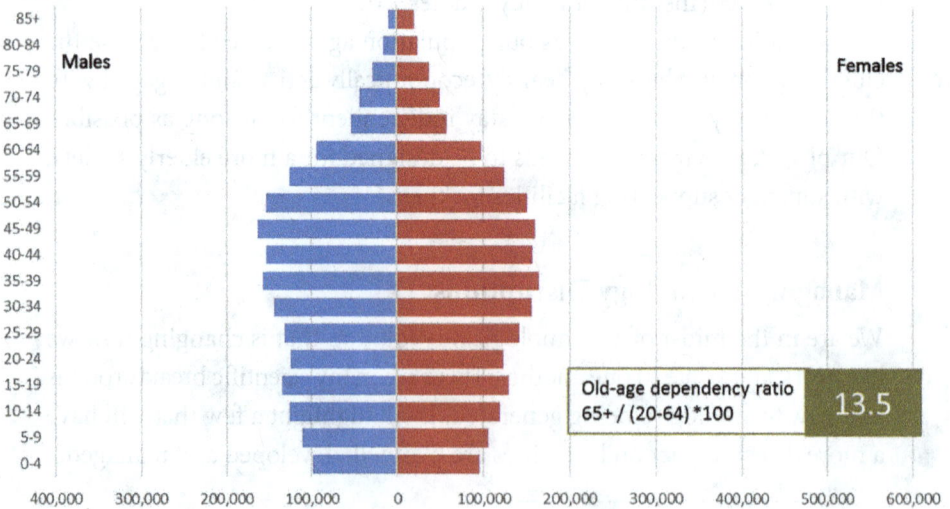

Males	Females

Old-age dependency ratio
65+ / (20-64) *100   **13.5**

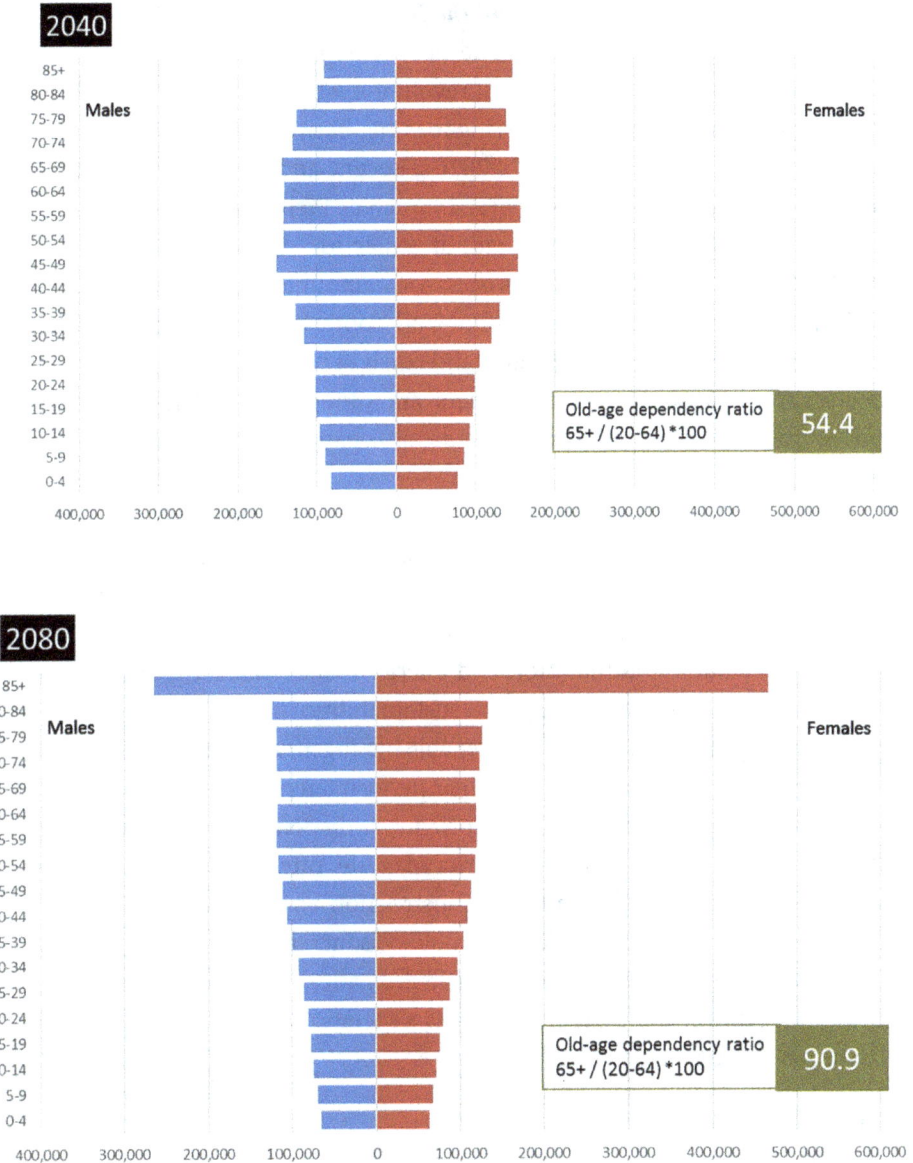

Figure 2: Singapore's ageing population
(Source: Institute of Policy Studies, Singapore Perspectives 2018 Conference Background Paper)

(a) Big data analytics, sensors and the Internet of Things (IoT)

Klaus Schwab, founder of the World Economic Forum, wrote that we are now undergoing a fourth industrial revolution which 'is characterised by a fusion of technologies that is blurring the lines between the physical, digital and biological spheres' (Schwab, 2016). Recent advances in information and communications technology (ICT), such as Web 2.0, cloud computing and sensor networking, have made it easier for the Internet of Things (IoT) to acquire, organise and process vast amounts of information. This information can be used to monitor and control the function of urban systems, and increase the efficiency and reach of urban services. It can help a city's residents, communities, leaders, and other stakeholders to become more informed and involved, and radically change how cities and homes are managed.

Many consumer technology companies are already moving into the smart home market. For example, Apple released its self-installed smart home system called Apple HomeKit in 2014, and Google launched Google Home, a brand of voice-activated smart speakers, in 2016. These systems deliver innovative building automation and energy management that maximise comfort, environmental quality, and sustainability.

Artificial intelligence (AI) will enable intelligent systems to collaborate with people and robots to improve their performance via machine learning. Pervasive robotic technology will provide indispensable support as our personal assistants and helpers in everyday life, offering wide application in the service, industrial, military, construction and medical sectors. For example, Human Augmentation Technology is increasingly used in Japan in healthcare as the population ages. AI will dramatically transform the way we live, work, move, and play, and we — as a society, nation, and city — need to be ready for this future.

(b) Next generation mobility

Digitisation and real-time information will make vehicular traffic more efficient, and enable an unprecedented degree of monitoring of urban mobility infrastructure. Autonomous Vehicles (AVs) will transport goods and people more efficiently and safely than manned vehicles over time. Each new autonomous vehicle is projected to replace 10 cars. The hope is that this will alleviate road congestion. If they are electric vehicles, oil use and attendant greenhouse gas emissions can be reduced by 71 per cent (Tonachel, 2018).

Airborne vehicles are also being explored in several countries. In 2016, Amazon famously patented a flying warehouse to dispatch drones from the sky. Another recent patent proposes a 'hive-like fulfilment centre' for drones. These multi-layered warehouses will be optimised for urban areas, occupying less land than the company's current single storey buildings.

Unmanned aerial vehicles can be programmed to deliver items such as food and medicines to homes, communicate with the power grid, and gather information about traffic, flooding, and other helpful data. Drones facilitate last-mile delivery, and may lead to a blurring of lines between retail and logistics space, by holding warehousing and delivery functions.

Drones could one day be used to transport people too. Uber is partnering NASA on its flying taxi project called Uber Elevate, which they are aiming to trial in Los Angeles, Dubai and Dallas-Fort Worth in 2020.

Such new technologies for movement will require us to rethink how we plan the city. For example, can we free up more road and traditional parking spaces, and repurpose them? Urban logistics will transform with AV trucks delivering goods at off-peak periods to reduce congestion. On the other hand, we need to address potential congestion caused by increased freight volumes, as a result of last-mile smaller deliveries arising from e-commerce. In addition to roads, we may now need to set out new regulations and pathways for drones to fly safely in the city.

(c) The sharing economy

On a broader scale, technology-enabled platforms like the smartphone and websites have produced an 'on-demand' or 'sharing' economy. These platforms can match supply and demand in a very accessible and low cost manner, creating new ways of consuming goods and services. For example, Airbnb facilitates the renting out of homes for short stays, and now has 150 million guests, threatening the hotel and hospitality sectors.

Uber and Grab have completely disrupted traditional taxi transport. Didi Chuxing in China operates 25 million daily rides with around four million drivers. Collection of data by their drivers enables Didi to use AI to even predict where riders are likely to want cars 15 minutes ahead of time, guessing right 85 per cent of the time and even learning the preferences of its passengers (Crabtree, 2018).

Workspaces can now be optimised and shared through co-working and flexible rental, reducing the need for traditional office space. In London, co-working spaces in 2016 accounted for some 8.5 per cent of the total take-up of space (Coleman, 2018). Demand for co-working spaces is expected to expand at an average rate of 10 to 15 per cent annually (Cushman & Wakefield and Corenet Global, 2017). Global players like WeWork are expanding in various cities. There are also numerous home grown operators like JustCo, Spacemob and Working Capitol, each trying to differentiate themselves through themed interiors and workstations. The current sector definitions of office, retail and industrial space will become more blurred, with more mixed uses co-locating as the nature of businesses changes. Developers and planners need to become more flexible and inventive to cater to these changes.

Online e-commerce has also affected the retail scene, putting pressure on traditional retail shops and malls. To attract footfall, stores now have to be 'experiential hubs' that provide entertainment and community offerings. Apple is a leader in this strategy; its stores are always packed with consumers testing products and interacting with store associates. Apple even calls its stores 'town squares', where people get together for events, classes and entertainment.

At the same time, online retailers like Alibaba and Amazon are adopting a 'new retail' strategy where they establish an offline presence by opening stores and pop-up spaces to test markets, get new product feedback, or persuade people browsing their sites to buy specific products (Urban Land Institute Asia Pacific and FGRT, 2018).

Online shopping has changed the logistics sector as the industry needs to get parcels delivered quickly to buyers. Spaces have to be allocated for buyers to collect and return parcels conveniently.

Addressing the Geo-Socialisation Trend

Geo-socialisation has been cited as the next trend in social networking (Frost & Sullivan, 2012). This is a geographically based type of socialisation, where social networking will rely on geographic services and capabilities — such as geo-coding and geo-tagging to allow social networks to connect users with people or events that match their interests, resulting in a more customised way of networking. For example, people can join a group chat at a sports event.

Businesses can also promote their geographically tagged services and respond to customer demand in real-time. For example, your mobile phone will point out interesting places, shops and restaurants near you, based on data of your user preferences, including receiving updates on promotions. This will drive new trends in digital marketing, socialising and networking. Interaction between individuals and organisations will further evolve through the use of Virtual Reality (VR) and Augmented Reality (AR).

Pokémon Go brought AR into the mainstream. Google's ARCore platform and Lenovo Phab 2 smartphone's AR features allow the phone to see and map the world around the user. AR can allow users to measure the size of a room and move virtual furniture around. VR will shake up retail. For example, Alibaba has launched a VR store called Buy+ that allows shoppers to wander in a VR mall complete with big-name stores. Such technologies would reduce the need for people to shop in a physical store.

Social networking also means that interactions are no longer limited by physical boundaries. From a social perspective, it requires planners to understand and redefine who 'neighbours' really are, and to think of new ways to promote communities and social bonding.

Planning in an Age of Rapid Change and Uncertainty

These trends and disruptions are all converging on Singapore. What should our urban responses to them be, so that we continue to be a liveable, resilient and dynamic city? In this lecture, I would like to raise some strategies for us to think about. I appreciate that many of these are already being studied by the various government agencies. Nevertheless, by highlighting holistically many of the ongoing efforts and sharing of ideas, I hope to contribute to a greater awareness of what it takes to anticipate needs and prepare Singapore for a better urban future.

Where Are We Today?

I highlighted in my first lecture that successful cities have shifted away from traditional blueprint plans to a long-term strategic planning approach. More importantly, successful implementation depends on the formulation of detailed implementation plans, which are then embedded in an institutionalised structure for execution.

Today, Singapore already adopts a long-term strategic planning approach. It is crucial that Singapore takes a long-term view when it plans. Given our land constraints, we need to develop strategies that will safeguard sufficient land to meet our development needs way into the future.

We now formulate strategic 'Concept Plans' with a long-term perspective of 40 to 50 years. Such plans focus on the strategic broad strokes rather than details, to safeguard land for all major land uses and key urban infrastructure (especially transport infrastructure) to support growth. The Concept Plan is reviewed roughly every 10 years to keep pace with changing needs, with additional reviews done by agencies internally where required. Singapore has had four Concept Plans, announced in the years 1971, 1991, 2001 and 2011. Phased medium-term plans are also worked out to help decision-makers make the necessary trade-offs between competing land uses and to prioritise infrastructure investments to support physical growth.

Concept Plan Reviews

The Concept Plan is cascaded to a statutory detailed Master Plan with a shorter horizon of about 15 years. The Master Plan maps out detailed land uses and the maximum plot ratio or density allowable for each site, and is reviewed every five years. The legislated Master Plan provides transparency and certainty to the private sector to guide their development and business decisions.

The formulation of the Concept Plan is a highly complex exercise that requires a whole-of-government effort. Inter-Ministry committees are formed, looking into matters of population, housing, transportation, commerce and

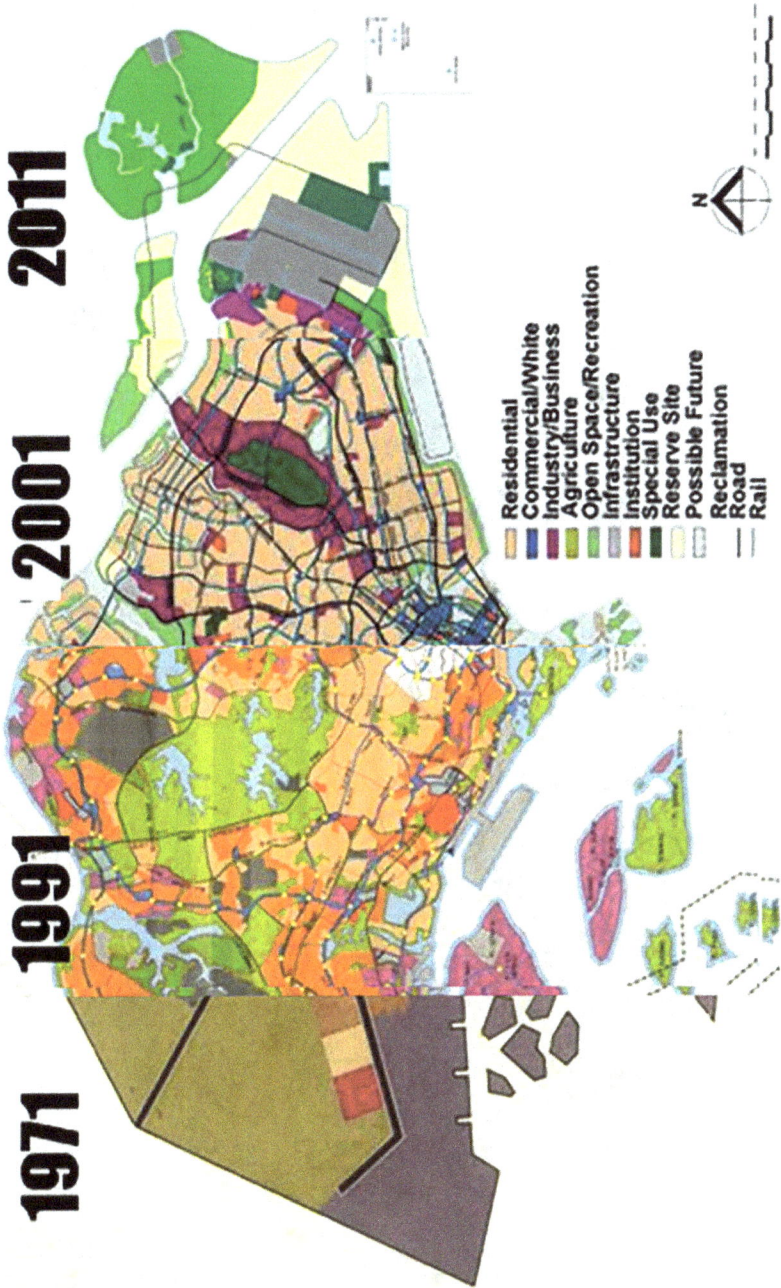

Figure 3: Singapore's Concept Plan reviews

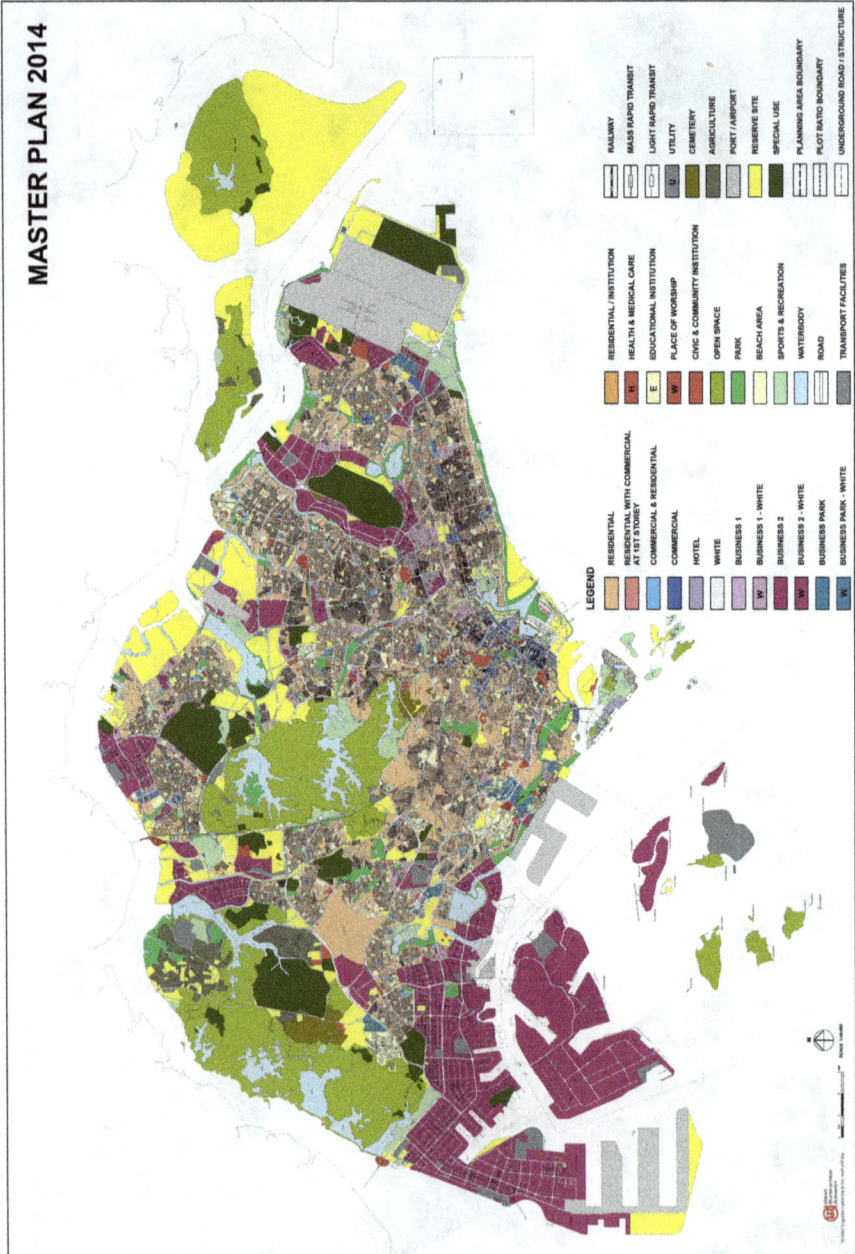

Figure 4: Singapore's Master Plan

CONCEPT PLAN REVIEW STRUCTURE

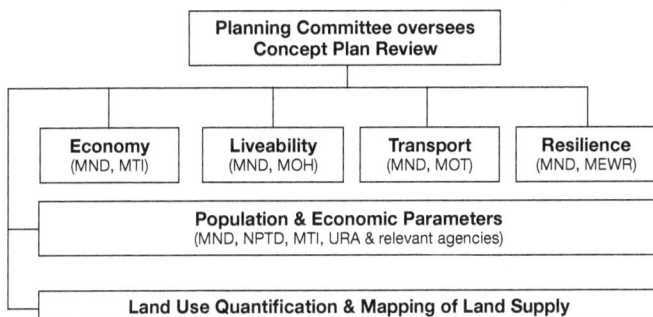

```
┌──────────────────────────────┐
│  Planning Committee oversees │
│     Concept Plan Review      │
└──────────────────────────────┘
```

| Economy (MND, MTI) | Liveability (MND, MOH) | Transport (MND, MOT) | Resilience (MND, MEWR) |

Population & Economic Parameters
(MND, NPTD, MTI, URA & relevant agencies)

Land Use Quantification & Mapping of Land Supply

Figure 5: Concept Plan review structure
(Source: Housing & Development Board)

industry, central area planning, environment, and recreation. The plans are not static; the assumptions and projections are revisited regularly and the strategies adjusted where necessary. This whole-of-government approach is especially critical as urban issues become increasingly complex and difficult trade-offs have to be made. The formation of the Prime Minister's Office Strategy Group in July 2015 is also timely, to identify and coordinate national priorities early and to translate them into policy action plans.[3] This institutionalised process has been a key factor in enabling many of our plans to be realised.

Going forward, what might be some strategies that we can consider in planning for our future? Let us examine some of these.

Adaptive Lifecycle Planning

Singapore is in transition into 'early middle age'. As our island becomes more built up in the next few decades, how can we secure land for future development?

---

[3] The PMO Strategy Group covers multiple policy areas such as strategic planning and futures, economy, land and liveability, population planning, marriage and parenthood, security and resilience, climate change, talent engagement and integration.

I would like to introduce the idea of 'adaptive lifecycle planning' — for a virtual cycle of land recovery, so as to enable a constant rejuvenation of Singapore for future generations.

Rejuvenation through recycling land

Similar to many mature cities, we have become built up over time and will be left with more brownfield than greenfield sites. This requires us to shift progressively into an 'urban redevelopment' mode. For an island city-state limited by our territorial waters, land for new development will come mainly from 'recycling' existing land and properties.

Given this, perhaps our long-term planning horizon should be stretched beyond the Concept Plan's current 40- to 50-year horizon to 100 years, to capture opportunities for potential redevelopment beyond the economic and useful lifespan of existing buildings and infrastructure. We would then be able to secure land for rejuvenation to meet the needs of future generations. Some may say that this proposal runs counter to the need to be flexible in a very uncertain world. However, I argue that 'lifecycle planning' would stretch our imagination and open us to future possibilities. If we think sufficiently long-term, the fixed constraints today, even large existing developments like airports, would depreciate sufficiently in the longer-term to allow for major moves in our plans. Taking a longer-term view will also enable us to factor in investments needed for costly infrastructure so that we can build up our fiscal resources over time.

This approach is not about formulating only one plan that is then locked in. Plans, such as the Concept Plan, would continue to be reviewed every five to 10 years. However, in the review of plans, we should take a very long-term planning horizon, keeping an eye on potential big moves that could be made in the longer term, so as not to foreclose future land use options when making shorter term decisions.

Our system of leasehold land is key to enabling such land rejuvenation to take place. For example, industrial land parcels, which are generally on 30- to 60-year leases, can be recovered when their leases end. The land can then be re-used to meet new needs and support new economic thrusts in the next lease cycle.

Figure 6: Port relocation from Tanjong Pagar to Pasir Panjang
(Source: Housing & Development Board)

We see many successful examples of such urban regeneration in the world. London and Bilbao are examples where port land, which is no longer needed, is redeveloped for new commercial, residential and cultural uses.

Similarly, we are relocating a large part of our port after some 50 years. PSA announced last year that it would be moving its Tanjong Pagar terminal to Pasir Panjang soon and, eventually, to the Tuas mega port. This new state-of-the-art port is slated to be operational from 2021 and fully ready by 2040. This shift will free up much of Singapore's southern waterfront for future residential, commercial, and leisure and recreational opportunities. In another example, the move of the military airbase at Paya Lebar to Changi in the future will free up 800 hectares for new developments.

These 'musical chair' moves are an essential strategy for rejuvenating our physical landscape. But to make changes to spatial patterns, we have to plan well ahead of time. A few large pockets of land need to be safeguarded to initiate these big moves.

Build adaptability into our planning

Being adaptable means that we should provide for 'modularity and flexibility' in our plans in view of future uncertainties. For example, even though we have safeguarded a large tract of land in Tuas for our port, it could be phased to retain strategic flexibility, in case projected demand for port activities does not pan out.

Building flexibility into our plans also requires us to be prepared to accommodate a larger population. Dr Liu Thai Ker[4] has advocated planning for a projected population of 10 million (Liu, 2016). His view has sparked public debate. No doubt, there will continue to be much discussion on what might be an appropriate population size for Singapore. This largely depends on whether we can find innovative urban solutions to sustain our good living environment, and on the level of acceptance by our citizenry.

Regardless of public sentiments, it is wise to plan for scenarios with varying population sizes. This would help planners to anticipate the types of infrastructure that will be needed, the appropriate densities to build on available land, and to work through the many difficult trade-offs in allocating land amongst competing uses. If the population growth does not materialise, we would have a happy situation of having more land buffer set aside and more choices in the use of land.

Develop 'no regrets' infrastructure and pursue land and space creation

When future demand is uncertain, how should we provide hard infrastructure which, once built, cannot be changed? One strategy is to plan for and invest in selected 'no regrets' infrastructure upfront, even if it might result in some redundancy and sub-optimisation. One example is the Mass Rapid Transit (MRT) rail network. Planning for more rail lines in anticipation of a larger population would enable us to safeguard the land for the rail corridors now before the city gets more built up. In fact, this was how we managed to build many of the existing MRT lines today. Our long-term planning approach meant that we had safeguarded the land corridors for many of our MRT lines since the 1970s. Sizing upfront a capacity with sufficient buffer for growth is

---

[4] Dr Liu Thai Ker was CEO of HDB (1979–1989), and CEO and chief planner of Urban Redevelopment Authority (1989–1992).

Figure 7: Land transport infrastructure
(Source: Land Transport Authority)

an important consideration because once the railway line and MRT station are built, any attempt to upgrade capacity is extremely costly, if not impossible.

A second example is land creation. Where possible, we should build up a land bank. An illustration of good planning foresight is the reclamation of land at Marina Bay since the 1970s in anticipation of the future growth of the city. This alleviated growth pressure on the existing city, and enabled us to conserve many of our historic districts. However, the extent to which we can reclaim land is limited by our territorial boundaries as we have to also preserve sea space to support our port functions. Therefore, we should explore other means of space creation as well.

JTC Corporation has successfully implemented the Jurong subterranean caverns for liquid storage. The government is looking into the development of more underground space. Opportunities exist in areas like the ground beneath Kent Ridge and the Singapore Science Park, where the soil formation underneath is suited for such underground construction. In collaboration with partner agencies, the Urban Redevelopment Authority (URA) is currently developing an Underground Master Plan, which it said would be announced in 2019.

We could also consider decking over large swathes of transport infrastructure, such as highways and MRT depots that take up extensive tracts of land. There are many successful examples where this has been done. Klyde Warren Park in Dallas was created by decking over highways. Millennium Park in Chicago and the new park at Hudson Yards in New York straddle a working rail yard.

Co-locating uses can also save land. The East Coast Integrated Depot, a new 36-hectare $3.2 billion depot will be built to house 220 trains for the Thomson-East Coast Line, East-West Line and Downtown Line. Said to be a world's first, the depot will also house 550 buses. By integrating the depots, the government expects to save 44 hectares of space, or about 60 football fields. It will be completed by 2024.

This strategy uses 'capital and technology' to overcome our limitations in land. The challenge is to find the right economic model to justify these expensive investments. For example, we were able to justify building the Marina Coastal Expressway underground because it would free up more prime land with access to the waterfront, and enhance overall land value. Similarly, decking over infrastructure use would create additional space and free up land elsewhere for other uses. Such projects should be seen as investments in our future.

Build greater flexibility in regulations and design

Planning regulations convert our land-use plans into working rules to steer developments towards specific planning objectives. Being adaptable is about building more flexibility into our zoning regulations to cater to the changing work patterns and market needs arising from the sharing and digital economy. When we planned Marina Bay, we introduced the 'white site' zone where we stipulated a minimum floor space for a specific use, such as a hotel, and then left it to the market to determine the remaining types of uses according to demand. The type of use could also be changed over time to meet evolving needs. More 'white sites' could be considered as we open up more mixed-use areas.

Recently, URA introduced an innovative zoning approach for the new Punggol Digital District — a district set aside for digital and cyber-security industries. Zoning rules would be applied at a district level instead of on individual parcels of land, giving developers more flexibility to mix uses.

Just as cities need to be adaptive, so should buildings be designed for greater flexibility. Reasonably sized floor plates, wider structural spans and sufficient floor to ceiling heights would allow a building to be converted and repurposed for a variety of uses over time. For example, Google's new Mountain View headquarters comprises a series of giant domes under which any number of structures — fit for any purpose — can be quickly assembled, making it completely programmable for any use case.

Infrastructure as an Integrated, Resilient and Intelligent Urban System

Develop an integrated national infrastructure plan

Many mature cities are ageing and suffering from a huge infrastructure gap. London recently formulated the £1.3 trillion (S$2.3 trillion) London Infrastructure Plan 2050, catering to an anticipated growth in London's population by 3.1 million between 2011 and 2050. This plan creates an integrated vision for London, encompassing sectors such as transport, green infrastructure, digital connectivity, water, energy and social infrastructure. It is the first-ever attempt to identify, prioritise and cost London's future infrastructure to 2050 (World Economic Forum, 2016). London also has an independent National Infrastructure Commission that advises the government on infrastructure development. It carries out assessments on the state of infrastructure, and takes a strategic approach by linking long-term priorities with short-term actions, so that infrastructure is seen as a dynamic system and not as a collection of silos (National Infrastructure Commission, n.d.).

Today, based on our Concept Plan's projections, individual agencies make provisions for key infrastructure such as those that provide transport, water, energy generation and waste management. Going forward, there is scope to rethink infrastructure as 'urban systems', and not just as specific stand-alone types of infrastructure, so that we can achieve closer integration and synergies between them.

As a small island city-state, we should work towards three important principles in our infrastructure provision:

a) To favour a circular rather than a linear model;

b) To adopt an integrated multi-function rather than a single function system; and

c) To build resilient and intelligent urban infrastructure.

This integrated way of developing infrastructure would support Singapore's National Climate Change plans to address climate change through a 'whole-of-nation' approach. The strategies include reducing emissions across sectors, building capabilities to adapt to the impact of climate change, harnessing green opportunities, as well as forging partnerships on climate change action (National Climate Change Secretariat, 2018).

One of the best examples of a circular system is the way in which the Public Utilities Board (PUB) has successfully closed the 'water loop'. Today, Singapore is designed as one giant, rain-water absorbing sponge. PUB has developed a whole network of drains, canals and underground storage tanks to capture rainfall. Through the introduction of the Deep Tunnel Sewerage System, PUB is also capturing all used water and is recycling it into NEWater, most of which is used by industries that require very clean water.

In our storm water management, we have started to 'green' grey infrastructure by introducing more sustainable alternatives. We use absorbent green spaces and wetlands for flood defence, which also create recreational and aesthetic value. Bishan-Ang Mo Kio Park and the Housing & Development Board (HDB) parks and ponds in Bidadari and Tengah towns all help to hold back water discharge after heavy rain. In addition, plants help to cleanse the water before it is discharged into drains and reservoirs, thus reducing the cost of water purification.

Our urban infrastructure should also act as a network of elements that is integrated and multi-functional, rather than serving a single function. Facilities could be creatively co-located to serve multiple uses. For example, Rotterdam, where certain neighbourhoods are as low as 6 metres below sea level, pioneered the construction of facilities like parking garages that become emergency reservoirs. Its dykes at Dakpark are integrated with other land uses such as a shopping centre and parking garage. The integrated facility also features one of the largest roof parks in Rotterdam.

Similarly, we should think of multi-functional strategies in say, land reclamation. For instance, in the future, reclamation of land along the East Coast and the Southern Waterfront, the reclamation could double up as a 'dam' — a coastal protection measure that protects inland low-lying areas along the East Coast. The reclaimed land could also be shaped to create more inland water bodies where heavy rainfall could be channelled, to prevent floods and double up as freshwater storage areas. These water bodies would provide opportunities for more beautiful waterfront housing and recreational areas.

Strengthen waste-energy-water nexus

We should pursue integrated infrastructure solutions that combine energy, waste and water, as they have the potential to provide benefits across multiple city systems. For example, while PUB has successfully recycled used water, the process consumes large amounts of energy. A recently announced PUB-National Environment Agency (NEA) project is a good example of how the waste-energy-water loop can be tapped to address the energy issue.

This is a $9.5 billion project comprising PUB's Tuas Water Reclamation Plant (TWRP) co-located with NEA's Integrated Waste Management Facility (IWMF), which will enable Singapore to reap the benefits of a water-energy-waste nexus while minimising land footprint. Essentially, electricity generated at IWMF from the incineration of trash will be supplied to TWRP for its operations. The TWRP will purify used water transported from the existing Deep Tunnel Sewerage System, into NEWater and industrial-grade water for reuse. At the same time, the de-watered sludge from TWRP will be incinerated at IWMF for electricity production. Food waste and used water sludge will also be co-digested, through a process called anaerobic digestion, where micro-organisms convert waste into biogas to enhance the overall thermal efficiency and electricity production at IWMF.

Intelligent infrastructure

We should combine engineering and data to enable a more intelligent approach to infrastructure so that we optimise energy generation and distribution, make our buildings smarter, and keep traffic flowing. Advances in sensors, controls and software can enable:

a) Increased intelligence and transparency, and provide the right information at the right time for informed decisions. With AI, we can move beyond normal monitoring of services towards predictive maintenance, where we can anticipate a problem and fix it before service is affected.

b) Integration: Information can be shared across systems and organisations to eliminate silos and optimise performance. For example, smart buildings can take on energy when it is cheap and plentiful, storing it first and then feeding it back to the grid when demand is high, thus optimising the use of energy.

Today, Singapore's infrastructure ecosystem, whilst efficient, may not be fully optimised. The above linkages between various infrastructure systems suggest that there may be merit to considering the development of a National Infrastructure Plan. This can then ensure that our long-term plans and vision are supported by timely infrastructure that takes a systems approach. Such a plan would identify opportunities to integrate and complement the various urban systems: food, energy, waste, water, transport, and greenery, and close the material and energy cycles thereby creating a circular ecosystem.

Deliver Well Managed and Liveable Density

With a growing population, living density in Singapore will increase from 11,000 persons per square kilometre to 13,700 persons per square kilometre, between now and 2030.[5] However, we need not fear densification if it is done well.

Densification takes place in cities because higher densities enable cities to absorb more people. Dense cities become engines of economic growth because they offer a larger market size for projects, attract talent for greater innovation, and provide the support and connectivity needed for businesses

---

[5] Living density takes into account only the land available for urban areas, and excludes land used for ports, airports, defence and utilities, amongst others.

to thrive. From a sustainability point of view, denser and compact cities also use less energy,[6] are more walkable, and help to make public transport options, waste disposal and management services more viable and efficient to operate.

However, we need to densify thoughtfully. Optimal density needs to be 'appropriate', and involves deliberate and decisive spatial planning and design strategies that make a city highly liveable. The following are some ways that can help to create liveable density.

Constellation of commercial centres to rebalance the urban pattern

To support economic growth, Singapore has developed two distinct economic hubs over time — our Central Business District (CBD) and the manufacturing hub in the west — which house some 70 per cent of our economic activities. Since Concept Plan 1991, we have adopted a 'constellation' of decentralised affordable spaces for commercial growth outside the city, to reduce traffic congestion in the city centre. As a result, today we have Tampines Regional Centre, which hosts many backend functions of banks, and new commercial sub-regional hubs like Paya Lebar and Novena, contributing to a better job to home ratio in the various regions.

Nonetheless, there is still high one-way travel demand from across the island towards the Central Area and West Region during peak hours. To reduce congestion and shorten commute time, URA and Land Transport Authority (LTA) are stepping up decentralisation efforts with a newly coined 'polycentric' approach. With more public housing being built in areas like Woodlands, Yishun, Punggol, and Jurong, there are opportunities to shift more commercial activities and jobs to newer areas. For example, to the north, we have the upcoming Woodlands Regional Centre, the North Coast Innovation Corridor that will include the Punggol Digital District and the

---

[6] The Global Commission on the Economy and Climate states that 'more compact, more connected city forms allow significantly greater efficiency and lower emissions per unit of economic activity' (Global Commission on the Economy and Climate, 2014). Lower-density cities of the United States (typically 10 persons per hectare or less) use about five times more energy per capita in gasoline than the cities of Europe, which are in turn about five times denser on average' (Urban Land Institute, and Centre for Liveable Cities, Singapore, 2013).

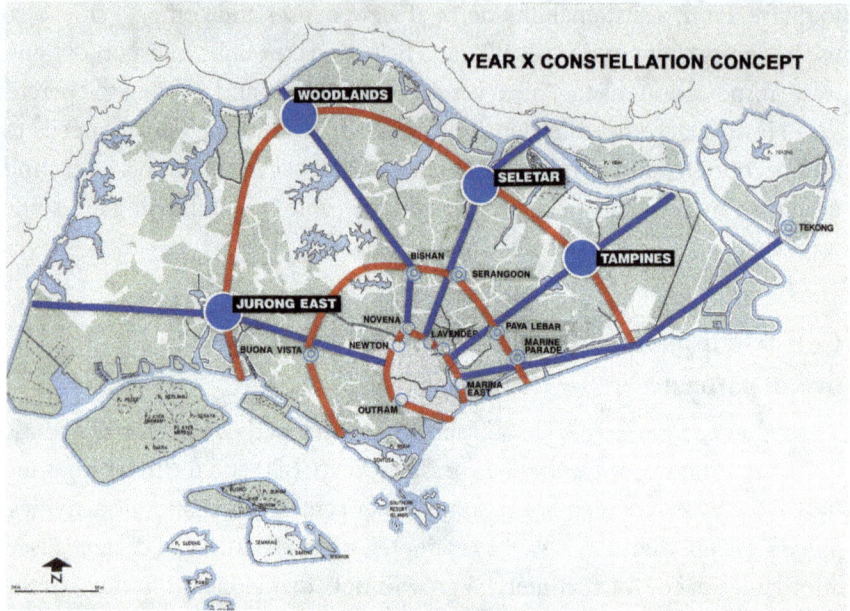

Figure 8: Concept Plan 1991's decentralisation strategy
(Source: Urban Redevelopment Authority. All rights reserved)

POLYCENTRIC CENTRES

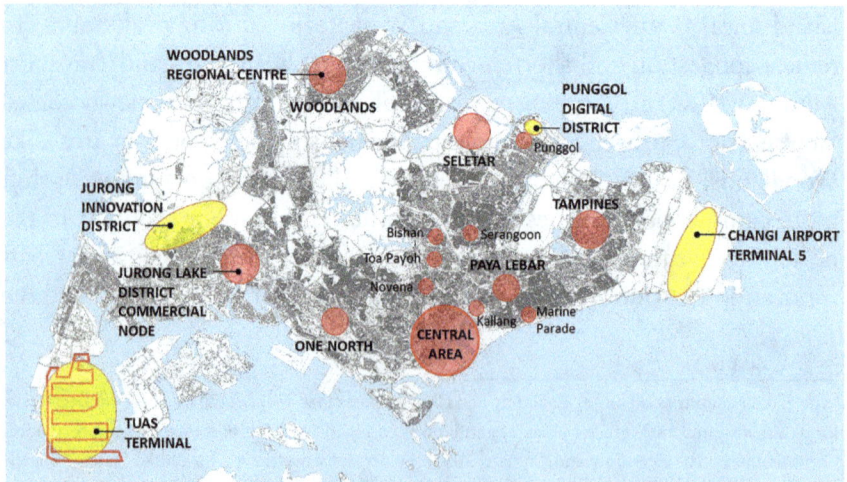

Figure 9: 'Polycentric' centres away from the CBD
(Source: Housing & Development Board)

new Singapore Institute of Technology. To the west, URA is expanding the Jurong Lake District Regional Centre into a new major western commercial node, to be potentially catalysed by the proposed high-speed rail terminus development. These commercial nodes will be well designed, mixed-use environments with amenities and more affordable rent, providing alternative premises for businesses.

The western region will also host the new PSA mega port in Tuas, and the Jurong Innovation District near Nanyang Technological University, providing more employment opportunities in those areas. In turn, more housing will be injected back into the Central Area, with new opportunities for development at the Southern Waterfront, Marina Bay and Marina East. This will improve the job to home ratio, and reduce cross-island travel.

Rethink urban mobility

Land-use planning must be supported by a good transport system. We have always adopted a 'transit-oriented' approach by encouraging the use of public transport that serves higher-density nodes. Singapore was one of the first cities to put in place policy measures, such as the Electronic Road Pricing (ERP) in the 1970s and the Certificate of Entitlement (COE) car quota scheme in 1990, to moderate car growth and to manage traffic congestion. Nonetheless, roads today still take up about 12 per cent of land — almost as much as the 14 per cent of land used for housing. To keep increasing the car population, which would in turn consume more land for roads, is simply not sustainable. Today, Singapore's public transport mode share is 67 per cent (Khaw, 2018). There is scope to push this higher when compared to cities like Hong Kong, where public transport accounts for 90 per cent of all total passenger trips (Transport and Housing Bureau, 2017). LTA has therefore set a target to improve our public transport mode share during peak periods to 75 per cent by 2030.

We must pursue alternative transportation modes beyond the car. In an interview in 2017, Ford's CEO Mark Fields said that 'the future of cities has almost nothing to do with cars…. The real problem… is how to prepare for a future in which people prefer to get around using all different modes of transportation: driverless cars, ride-sharing, train, bus, bicycle and on foot'[7].

In Singapore, there is now a big push towards a 'car-lite' society. Last year, LTA announced that it will adopt a zero growth car policy. The idea is to shift increasingly towards 'mobility as a service', rather than having individually owned cars. LTA is overseeing pilot programmes for car sharing and AVs to yield greater efficiency and safety so that road space can be reduced. Car parking supply is being tightened, particularly within the city core. Last year, URA exhibited possible ideas for future neighbourhoods at Bayshore and Holland Plain, and architects mooted the idea of reducing car parks by 50 per cent in those districts.

A 'car-lite policy' will need to be supported by alternative affordable and convenient modes of transport. LTA is investing heavily in rail and doubling the rail network from 178 km to 360 km by 2030 (Land Transport Authority, 2013). LTA has also added on some 1,000 buses to its fleet (Land Transport Authority, 2017).

Many kilometres of cycling tracks are being developed to encourage more people to cycle. In 2017, LTA passed the Active Mobility Bill to allow the use of bicycles and Personal Mobility Devices (PMDs) on public paths. We now have bike sharing too. It is still early days to conclude whether cycling will take off in a big way and whether we can get cyclists, pedestrians and drivers to co-exist harmoniously. In the meantime, the cycling network will continue to be expanded to improve convenience and connectivity.

To reduce congestion, there is a need to explore more sustainable urban logistics solutions too. JTC is looking at incorporating a central distribution centre at Jurong Innovation District (JID) where goods are stored and handled, and a dedicated road network for the delivery of goods to companies. The government is also looking into an island-wide federated parcel locker network to ease the last-mile delivery challenges.

Use of unmanned aerial vehicles (UAV) is likely to increase. For example, Airbus's Skyways project aims to provide efficient, seamless delivery of small

---

[7] Ford created Ford Smart Mobility in March 2016, bought Chariot, shuttle service based in San Francisco, and partnered bike-sharing company, Motivate, to launch its own bike-share service by end-2017 (Weller, 2017).

parcels via drones across the National University of Singapore campus. Such initiatives require us to consider designing cities that cater to 3D mobility, which includes safe pathways and landing for UAVs and regulations to ensure safety. In fact, Nanyang Technological University's Air Traffic Management Research Institute is developing a traffic management system for drones called the Traffic Management of Unmanned Aircraft Systems. Air traffic lanes are designated by using 'virtual fences' to reroute drones around restricted geographical locations, thus enabling hundreds of UAVs to fly efficiently and safely at any one time (Nanyang Technological University, 2016).

Build a city of greenery and water

Our agencies, such as URA, National Parks Board (NParks), PUB and HDB have done much to achieve balanced urban development. Notably, they have cultivated lush greenery and maintained water bodies throughout the island to great effect. There are some 360 parks today and more will be built. Singapore has safeguarded large swathes of nature reserves right in the heart of the island, and national parks such as the Botanic Gardens and Gardens by the Bay within the city centre. The new Jurong Lake Gardens will be the first national garden in the heartlands and next to the new western region commercial node.

We are constantly creating the 'illusion of space' through innovative 'multiplication' effects. For example, URA successfully created a large linear hill park simply by connecting Mount Faber and Kent Ridge Park with architecturally striking bridges that straddle roads. Our park connector network has enabled greater access to cycling and jogging trails, with links to multiple parks and coastal areas.

The rail corridor will soon become another well-loved space for a quick getaway from the hustle and bustle of the city. Imagine the possibility of linking the rail corridor to surrounding attractions such as historic areas and parks, with offshoots to interesting neighbourhoods, food havens, nature and biodiversity areas. It would indeed be a creative way to expand our leisure space multi-fold in this small island.

At the building level, we are replacing the greenery lost to developments on the ground, through the creation of new land by way of sky terraces and sky gardens. Water elements are weaved into the urbanscape using water sensitive urban design comprising bioswales and rain gardens. By planting the right plants, we are bringing back greater biodiversity and attracting the return of wildlife such as otters, hornbills and other birds.

More edible gardens and urban farms

One area that we could explore is to increase the amount of food produced in Singapore. Aside from more productive commercial farms, we could explore urban farming by the community. Recently, NParks announced that it would encourage more people to adopt edible gardening, viz. the planting of edible fruits and vegetables. HDB, in its planning of the new Tengah town, has weaved in large linear greens. We could explore the introduction of small-scale urban farming, roping in community groups and social enterprises.

Develop 'people cities' using excellent design

Successful, liveable and distinctive cities are 'people-focused'. They go beyond functionality to build identity, image and great environmental quality through good design. We need to develop a pervasive culture of design excellence from macro urban design to the smallest details of buildings and city infrastructure. A well-executed juxtaposition of high and lower blocks can provide both relief and a more interesting and unique skyline for the city. Well-designed, high-density developments interwoven with landscaped greenery, water bodies and public spaces, conveniently served by facilities, can produce a high-quality living environment.

Great public spaces encourage community interaction and activities, and bring vibrancy to a city. Beyond the design of great public spaces, we should promote effective place-making and programming to encourage greater vibrancy and community interaction. We have already been successful in generating much activity in areas like Marina Bay and the Civic District. Roping in stakeholders to take ownership of place-making activities is essential to sustain such activities.

Good urban design will help to shape a good environment and enable us to plan well for an ageing population. We need to embrace universal design, mixed uses and new typologies to enable convenient movement,

Figure 10: 'Fosterito' subway entrance (left) and subway station (right) by Norman Foster in Bilbao

access to facilities, and social interaction. I will cover more of this issue in my next lecture.

I would also appeal for greater attention to be paid to the quality of design of our public spaces and urban infrastructure. Increasingly, our urban infrastructure is creeping into our crowded streetscape, and if we are not careful, could mar the visual experience of our city. Careful attention must be paid to the design of larger urban structures such as the increasing numbers of ventilation buildings, and MRT stations and entrances. There are also miles of overhead ramps, pedestrian bridges, linkways and multiple signage that crop up along streets. We need to bring some order to these since we experience a city largely at the street level.

We can take a leaf from cities that have lovingly nurtured a design culture that looks at all aspects of public infrastructure. For example, Bilbao commissioned Norman Foster to build the signature 'fosteritos' that are the glass entrances to all its subway stations.[8] Barcelona has attractive boulevards such as the Passeig de St Joan Boulevard, where the scale and design of sidewalks, trees, signage, lamp posts and street furniture are all beautifully coordinated. Transport facilities can be beautiful if we put some thought into careful design before we build.

To be a people-oriented city, we need to be mindful of conserving built heritage to retain social memories. In the case of Singapore, it is a difficult balance deciding the extent to which we should keep built heritage and

---

[8] See Lecture I in this collection.

places while ensuring we have sufficient land for development. It is about finding a sustainable economic model that will enable the built heritage to be used purposefully, so that owners can afford to upkeep heritage buildings. Inevitably, the debate on how much to conserve and what to conserve will continue, and perhaps this is a healthy sign that people do care about heritage. On the whole, Singapore has developed one of the most comprehensive urban conservation programmes in Southeast Asia, having conserved some 7,000 buildings and structures, with many of the areas conserved as entire districts. In fact, in 2006, the Urban Land Institute recognised URA's conservation programme as one that 'balances free market economics with cultural conservation' (URA, Centre for Liveable Cities, and the Embassy of France in Singapore, 2016).[9]

Reimagining the City from the Internet Up

During a recent visit to New York, I met with the people behind Sidewalk Labs, Alphabet Inc.'s smart city incubator that imagines, designs, tests, and builds urban innovations to help cities meet their challenges. Its stated goal at the time was 'reimagining cities from the Internet-up' (Doctoroff, 2016).

Singapore, too, has its Smart Nation ambitions, to 'support better living, stronger communities, and create more opportunities for all' (Centre for Liveable Cities, 2016). As a small, integrated city-state, Singapore is well poised to harness smart technology in a big way. It can help us to overcome our limited resources and make the leap to more innovative and effective urban solutions.[10] For a start, the intention is to focus on five key domains that will have significant impact on the citizen and society — covering transport, home and environment, business productivity, health and enabled ageing, and government services (Woo, 2017).

---

[9] Singapore's conservation programme was awarded the Urban Land Institute's Award for Excellence: Asia Pacific in 2006.

[10] At the World Economic Forum (WEF) 2016 meeting, UBS put together a ranking of countries most likely to benefit the most from the next industrial revolution, based on a combined metric of the flexibility of their labour markets, how skilled their workers are, how prepared the education system is for change, and the legal system. Singapore was ranked second after Switzerland (Moshinsky, 2016).

GOAL

SINGAPORE AS A LEADING DIGITAL
ECONOMY WHICH CONTINUALLY REINVENTS ITSELF

STRATEGIC
PRIORITIES

ACCELERATE	COMPETE	TRANSFORM
DIGITALISING INDUSTRIES	INTEGRATING ECOSYSTEMS	INDUSTRIALISING DIGITAL
Accelerate digitalisation of existing sectors	Grow Singapore's competitiveness by fostering new ecosystems, enabled by digital	Developing the next gen digital industry as an engine of growth

ENABLERS

TALENT

RESEARCH & INNOVATION

POLICY, REGULATIONS & STANDARDS

PHYSICAL & DIGITAL INFRASTRUCTURE

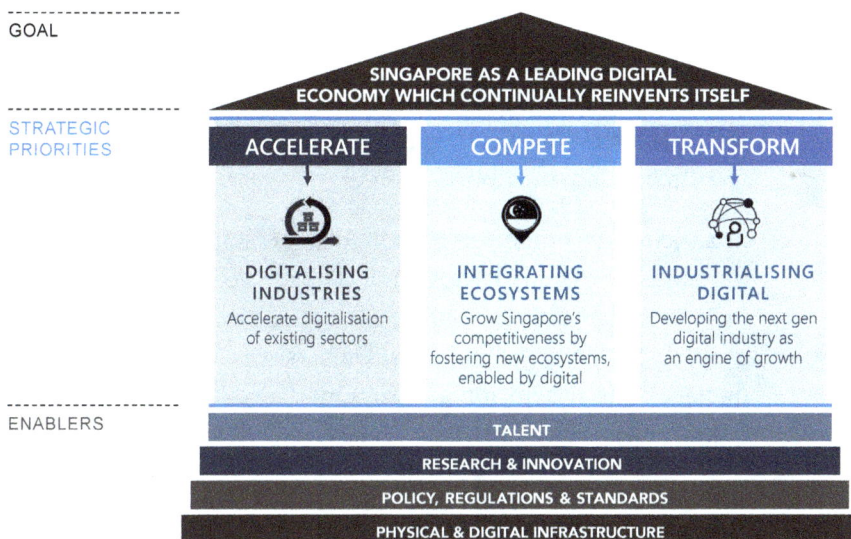

Figure 11: Singapore Digital (SG:D) Digital Economy Framework for Action
(Source: Infocomm Media Development Authority)

The following are some of the more significant applications that hold
promise in providing new possibilities for the physical management of cities.

Smarter transport

With more than one million vehicles on the road and four million daily
bus rides, Singapore can deploy smart technologies to optimise the use of
our limited space for more efficient, safe, and reliable transportation. Some
interesting ongoing initiatives include:

a) Mobility on Demand pilots such as the Delphi Automotive Systems
    and nuTonomy vehicles being piloted at the One-North test bed.
    LTA will introduce self-driving buses at Punggol, Tengah and Jurong
    Lake District over the next few years. Self-driving vehicles also
    hold great potential for freight transportation as they can address
    manpower challenges and ease traffic congestion during peak hours
    by operating at night.

b) LTA has also analysed anonymised data from commuters' fare cards and identified commuter hotspots to manage bus fleets.[11] A next generation Electronic Road Pricing system slated for 2020 will collect real-time data to provide a more accurate picture of the real-time traffic situation.

c) In anticipation of the use of more drones, Singapore has already introduced the Unmanned Aircraft (Public Safety and Security) Bill in 2016, which aims to regulate the use of drones with a clear set of rules. Nanyang Technological University is developing a traffic management system for drones. One-North has recently been designated as Singapore's first drone estate.

Home and environment

Smart initiatives for home and environment focus on applications that improve liveability, sustainability and safety of the urban habitat, and enable us to bring more reliable and efficient services to our residents. HDB has developed a Smart HDB Town Framework that focuses on harnessing digital technology. I will provide more details of these initiatives in my third lecture.

Health and enabling ageing

Assistive technology, analytics and robotics can be deployed to support ageing residents and healthcare services. Such technology can help the shift towards home-based healthcare rather than institutionalised care. This would relieve the fiscal and manpower burden, and the large land take required if we were to provide more new hospitals and nursing homes as the population ages.

From Digital-Age to En-Gage

While technical professionals and policy-makers pursue the latest technological advances and the smart applications to manage the city, we

---

[11] Arrival times of buses are tracked using sensors installed in over 5,000 vehicles. With such information, there has been a 92 per cent reduction in the number of bus services with crowding issues, and average waiting time on popular services have been shortened by three to seven minutes (Smart Nation Singapore, 2018).

must remember that, ultimately, we are planning for our people. A more participatory approach to planning will enable us to better understand what they want and whether our plans are meeting their needs. A co-creation process can help to harness the ideas and enterprise of the community, and promote joint ownership of our environment.

Many of the proposed initiatives will not be successful without the support and cooperation of our people. For example, while transport experts can pronounce a 'car-lite' policy, car owners need to be persuaded to give up their cars and switch to alternative transport modes. As we introduce more bicycles and PMDs, there needs to be more consideration among cyclists, PMD users and pedestrians — so as to share the same pathways safely and harmoniously. Extensive engagement and education is needed to persuade citizens to adopt a code of conduct.

Our attempt to build a low-carbon and climate-resilient society will fail without the participation of our people. Businesses need to be brought on board to embrace innovations and new business models in emerging concepts. These include green growth (i.e., aligning climate mitigation and economic progress) and the circular economy (i.e., keeping products in use for as long as possible, thereby minimising resource use, waste, and emission). Green cities require 'green' citizens who have a 'sustainability ethos' ingrained in their daily lives. In Yokohama, residents are able to recycle and sort out their trash into 15 types. Much needs to be done in Singapore to get more citizen buy-in to better manage our personal use of energy, water and resources.

Strong Research and Innovation

Today, we are turning to research, innovation and technology as critical tools to develop urban solutions. The Singapore government has committed some $19 billion for the Research, Innovation and Enterprise (RIE) 2020 Plan from 2016 to 2020. Of this, some $900 million has been set aside for the Urban Solutions and Sustainability domain (covering energy, water, land and liveability). In 2017, the Ministry of National Development launched a Cities of Tomorrow (CoT) R&D programme, setting aside $150 million to fund research and development towards building a more liveable, sustainable and resilient city for the future.

There is also increasing recognition of the City as a network of Complex Urban Systems. This requires us to understand how each urban system and infrastructure system relates to the other, and the cause and effect between the different systems. This is necessary if we want a resilient city, and to avoid any risk of single-point failures.

However, the city is not just about efficiency, engineering and technology.

Towards a More Humanistic Approach to Urban Science

In a recent discussion I had with a group of eminent experts on how we should develop and manage cities, an important point made was that we must avoid a 'hegemony of infrastructure' in our approach to cities. Cities should not only be viewed as 'machines' with a focus on efficiency and cost effectiveness through engineering- or technology-based infrastructure solutions. Technology should not be allowed to alienate people.

Cities must be developed with a view towards clear societal goals and outcomes, such as achieving a good quality of life, strong communities, and a sustainable environment to conserve resources for future generations. Technology and infrastructure solutions are but enablers for our human-centred development goals.

It follows that our research agenda should put people at its centre, and we should incorporate behavioural sciences and social studies, so that we understand the factors that could affect or drive human behaviour. For example, to guide the development of future transport plans, we need to understand the factors that influence the choice of homes and work, which in turn may be linked to the choice of mode of transport. To plan for liveable density, we must ask what fosters and influences the sense of well-being — both spatial and non-spatial factors. What types of activities and spaces are more likely to encourage use and interaction? Beyond traditional data collection using surveys and censuses, we should shift towards harnessing big data, which can be gathered through platforms such as social media, sensors and mobile phone data, to give us better insights on psychological, social and spatial behaviours.

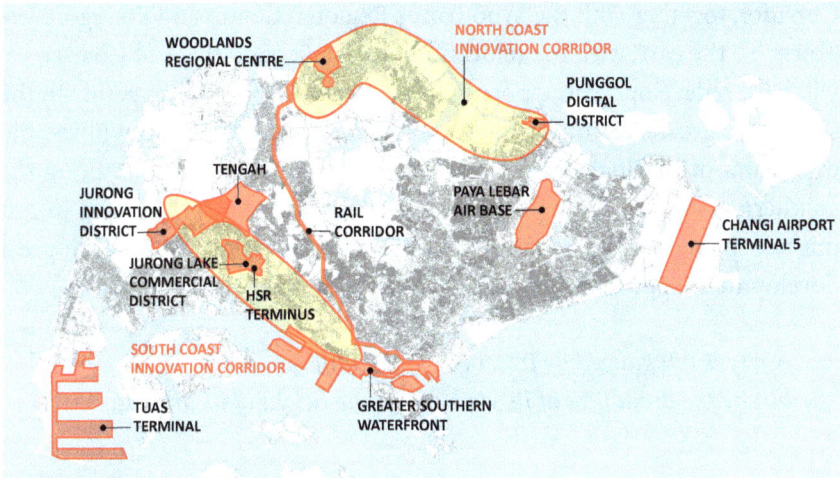

Figure 12: Upcoming major projects
(Source: Housing & Development Board)

We have generally been efficient over the years in applying many hardware solutions to deal with our urban challenges, but there is much more to be done to better understand the 'software' of cities. This is particularly important as society becomes more diverse. For this reason, stakeholder engagement has featured more prominently in our development and planning processes. The success of many of our policies and urban solutions would depend on how well we can take into account, nudge, and shape human and social behaviour and responses.

Dream Audaciously

Indeed, many mega trends that will affect our future urban environment are descending upon us. But given that we are already adopting a long-term whole-of-government approach and greater efforts to engage and work with our people, we are in a good position to prepare for future changes.

We are in an exciting time where, over the next few decades, several extensive development projects are lined up for development. To the west, there is the new large western commercial district at Jurong East and the Jurong Innovation District together with the new Tengah town and the Tuas Mega Port. To the north, we will build up the North Coast Innovation

Corridor, together with the Woodlands Regional Centre and Punggol New Town. To the east, with the relocation of Paya Lebar airbase to Changi, we will have redevelopment opportunities. Changi Airport will expand. To the south, the greater Southern Waterfront on vacated port land will see the expansion of Marina Bay, with a new waterfront development along the southern coast. All these projects will give us many opportunities to test out new planning ideas, urban solutions and technology. With such great development opportunities, we should dare to dream audaciously.

> *A city is not gauged by its length and width …*
> *but by the broadness of its vision, and the height of its dreams.*

— Herb Caen

With thoughtful, people-centred planning, strong science and technology, and an innovative spirit, Singapore can continue to transform and shine as a 'rock star' in urban solutions.

References

Centre for Liveable Cities Singapore. (2016). Lessons from New York for Singapore's Smart Nation journey. Retrieved from https://www.clc.gov.sg/docs/default-source/commentaries/lessons-from-new-york-for-singapore-smart-nation-journey.pdf

Coleman, R. (2018, January 23) Boom in UK co-working as flexible workspace take-up triples in top cities. Cushman & Wakefield. Retrieved from http://www.cushmanwakefield.co.uk/en-gb/sitecore/content/news/uk/2018/01/coworking-report

Committee on the Future Economy. (2017, February 8). Report of the Committee on the Future Economy: Pioneers of the next generation. Retrieved from https://www.gov.sg/~/media/cfe/downloads/mtis_full%20report.pdf

Crabtree, J. (2018, February 9). Didi Chuxing took on Uber and won. Now it's taking on the word. Wired UK. Retrieved from https://www.wired.co.uk/article/didi-chuxing-china-startups-uber

Cushman & Wakefield and Corenet Global. (2017, April). Co-working: Understanding the ongoing revolution. Retrieved from https://f.datasrvr.com/fr1/717/12758/Coworking_Report_FINAL.pdf

Doctoroff, D. L. (2016, November 30). Reimagining cities from then Internet up. Medium — Sidewalk Talk. (Blog). https://medium.com/sidewalk-talk/reimagining-cities-from-the-internet-up-5923d6be63ba

Frost & Sullivan Market Insight, (2012, May 29). Six degrees apart: Geo socialization: The next trend in social networking. Retrieved from http://www.frost.com/prod/servlet/market-insight-print.pag?docid=260990299#top

Global Commission on Climate and Economy. (2014). The new climate economy report 2014: Better growth better climate. Retrieved from https://newclimateeconomy.report/2014/overview/

Herb Caen. (2010, October 31). A city is like San Francisco, not a faceless 'burb. SFGate. Retrieved from https://www.sfgate.com/entertainment/article/A-city-is-like-San-Francisco-not-a-faceless-burb-3168435.php

Institute of Policy Studies. (2017). Harnessing Singapore's longevity dividends: The generational economy. Singapore Perspectives 2018 Conference Background Paper. Retrieved from http://lkyspp2.nus.edu.sg/ips/wp-content/uploads/sites/2/2017/11/SP2018-background-paper_180118.pdf

Khaw, B. W. (2018, March 7). Speech by Minister Khaw Boon Wan at the Ministry of Transport's Committee of Supply Debate 2018. Ministry of Transport. Retrieved from http://www.mot.gov.sg/news-centre/news/Detail/speech-by-minister-khaw-boon-wan-at-the-ministry-of-transport-s-committee-of-supply-debate-2018/

Land Transport Authority (Singapore). (2013). More connections: Expanding our rail network. In Land Transport Master Plan 2013 (19–26). Singapore: Land Transport Authority. Retrieved from https://www.lta.gov.sg/content/dam/ltaweb/corp/PublicationsResearch/files/ReportNewsletter/LTMP2013Report.pdf

Land Transport Authority (Singapore). (2017). Better bus services. In New Journeys: Land Transport Authority Annual Report 2016/2017 (40-41). Singapore: Land Transport Authority. Retrieved from https://www.lta.gov.sg/content/dam/ltaweb/corp/PublicationsResearch/files/AnnualReports/1617/LTA%20ANNUAL%20REPORT%202016-2017.pdf

Liu, T. K. (2016). Intelligent urban planning in Singapore: Practice and insights. In Challenges and Reforms in Urban Governance: Insights from the Development Experience of China and Singapore (96). Singapore: Centre for Liveable Cities Singapore and Development Research Center of the State Council of the People's Republic of China.

Mercer (2017, March 31). Vienna tops Mercer's 19th quality of living ranking. Press release. Retrieved from https://www.mercer.com/newsroom/2017-quality-of-living-survey.html

Moshinsky, B. (2016, March 14). Ranked: The 16 countries set to benefit most from the next industrial revolution. Business Insider UK. Retrieved from http://uk.businessinsider.com/countries-set-to-benefit-the-most-from-the-next-industrial-revolution-2016-3/?IR=T

Nanyang Technological University. (2016, December 28). NTU to develop traffic management solutions so drones can fly safely in Singapore airspace.

National Climate Change Secretariat, Strategy Group, Prime Minister's Office. (2018, February 20). Impact of climate change on Singapore. Retrieved from https://www.nccs.gov.sg/climate-change-and-singapore/national-circumstances/impact-of-climate-change-on-singapore

National Infrastructure Commission (United Kingdom). (n.d.) What we do. Retrieved from https://www.nic.org.uk/what-we-do/

Schwab, K. (2016, January 14). The fourth industrial revolution: What it means and how to respond. Economic Forum. Retrieved from https://www.weforum.org/agenda/2016/01/the-fourth-industrial-revolution-what-it-means-and-how-to-respond/

Singapore Department of Statistics, (2018, July 6). Understanding old-age support ratio. Retrieved from https://www.singstat.gov.sg/modules/infographics/old-age-support-ratio

Smart Nation Singapore. (2018, June 26). Open data and analytics for urban transformation. Retrieved from https://www.smartnation.sg/initiatives/Mobility/open-data-and-analytics-for-urban-transportation

Strategy Group, Prime Minister's Office, Singapore Department of Statistics, Ministry of Home Affairs, Immigration & Checkpoints Authority, and Ministry of Manpower. *Population in Brief 2017*. Retrieved from https://www.strategygroup.gov.sg/docs/default-source/default-document-library/population-in-brief-2017.pdf

Tonachel, L. (2015, September 17). Study: Electric vehicles can dramatically reduce carbon pollution from transportation, and improve air quality. Natural Resources Defense Council. Retrieved from https://www.nrdc.org/experts/luke-tonachel/study-electric-vehicles-can-dramatically-reduce-carbon-pollution

Transport and Housing Bureau. (2017, June). Public Transport Strategy Study. Hong Kong Transport and Housing Bureau. Retrieved from https://www.td.gov.hk/filemanager/en/publication/ptss_final_report_eng.pdf

Urban Land Institute, and Centre for Liveable Cities, Singapore. (2013). 10 principles for liveable high-density cities: Lessons from Singapore. Singapore: Urban Land Institute and Centre for Liveable Cities, Singapore. Retrieved from http://uli.org/wp-content/uploads/ULI-Documents/10PrinciplesSingapore.pdf

Urban Land Institute Asia Pacific and FGRT. (2018, January 10). ULI Hong Kong: The tenant of the future flash report. Retrieved from https://asia.uli.org/wp-content/uploads/sites/126/ULI-Documents/FGRT18_2.pdf

Urban Redevelopment Authority Singapore, Centre for Liveable Cities, and the Embassy of France in Singapore. (2016, May). Heritage and sustainable urbanism: Case studies from France, Singapore and the region. (Singapore: Centre for Liveable Cities).

Weller, C. (2017, January 31). Ford's CEO says the future of cities has almost nothing to do with cars. Business Insider Singapore. Retrieved from https://www.businessinsider.sg/ford-ceo-future-of-cities-nothing-to-do-with-cars-2017-1/

Woo, J. J. (2017). Singapore Smart Nation initiative: A policy and organisational perspective. Lee Kuan Yew School of Public Policy. Retrieved from https://lkyspp.nus.edu.sg/docs/default-source/case-studies/singapores_smart_nation_initiative

World Economic Forum. (2016, April). Enablers for adopting new models for urban services. In Adopting new models for urban services (33–34). Geneva: World Economy Forum. Retrieved from http://www3.weforum.org/docs/WEF_Urban-Services.pdf

Question-and-Answer Session
Moderated by Professor Chan Heng Chee

Professor Chan Heng Chee (CHC): Thank you very much, Dr Cheong, for that breath-taking, brilliant and comprehensive talk. What you have done is to bring together what we need to think about when we talk of our urban future, highlighting the challenges and drivers of change.

Now, I have to say, you startled me when you said that you wanted to start planning with a long horizon — a hundred years! And I thought, are you serious? Because the very drivers you named, such as technology, I do not think we can predict technology beyond even 20 years, 25 years. The smartphone completely changed the way we lived back in 2007. To talk of a hundred years, what does that mean?

I remember a conference I had organised on Lee Kuan Yew and the physical transformation of Singapore, at which we learnt that 50 years ago, Mr Lee had, in fact, decided how Singapore was to be planned. 'This is where housing would be, this is where the airport would be, and this is the Central Business District.' I am told by planners that it is amazing how relevant and applicable his basic plan has been. But planning for a hundred years is very different. As a political scientist, I note that, in that time frame, we had seen a British government and a Japanese government; we tried to get an independent future and became part of Malaysia; then we came out of Malaysia and now, we are what we are. Is it too ambitious to plan for a hundred years?

Dr Cheong Koon Hean (CKH): I was trying to be provocative. But first, let me clarify. When you plan for a hundred years, it does not mean that you make one plan and then you stop planning altogether. That is not the planning process. It is not about a 'planned city' but about a 'city that continually plans'. There is a difference, because a planned city would be in blueprint mode and within five years, the plan is already outdated. It is more about the process of planning and thinking very long-term. I agree with you that technology will change, and you cannot predict the future. There are, however, certain things that do not change so easily. Your MRT lines, your airports, your port, the reservoirs — these are not so easy to change.

If you look at the plan of Singapore, first developed in the 1960s and early 1970s — when experts like Otto Koenigsberger came through the United Nations to help us with our urban development and renewal plan — the structure of the plan is still largely the same. It has not changed that much. So, the backbone does not change that much. Of course, there will be other changes; for example, maybe we might not need as much space as we thought we did. But then, given that this is Singapore, you are talking about a country that is a city-state. If it were the United States of America or Australia, I would not worry as much about planning. They can just move to a new city if need be. But we cannot.

Thinking ahead gives you potential levers to make very big moves. You need to be able to think ahead of the possibilities. Many people feel very restricted about looking very far because they say, oh, the building is there, the road is there. But nothing lasts forever. A building will grow old and will need to be replaced. From an economic point of view, every building and infrastructure will depreciate over time. Given that you are a city-state, with no hinterland where you can build elsewhere, you do have to think about the recycling of land.

Even though you plan for a hundred years, you would also continue to have at least another 10 concept plan reviews in that time. So you are continually planning, but you always need to have that long-term horizon.

Two other very important things to bear in mind: if you want to do these 'musical chairs' moves of shifting major infrastructure facilities, you need to safeguard huge chunks of land so that you can move entire chunks. Second, they are very expensive to do, so you may not have the money now, but if you tell me that, in 30 years, I need to do this, then a good government would think about how to build up the resources for that to happen. And this does happen — the port is moving! It has happened before, when we moved the airport to Changi, remember?

CHC: Thank you, Koon Hean. Now, I invite the audience to ask questions, but I will group the questions, so that she answers two to three questions at the same time.

Participant: This idea of decking over the highways is a great one, and it seems to be catching on in many countries. How about Singapore? For example, with landscape decked over Orchard Road, we can create a lot of activities. If you can build this land stack from one end to another, and if it proves to be successful, we can continue this idea to Little India, Bras Basah, Shenton Way and Chinatown. I would like your views on this, please.

Participant: I want to ask specifically about Orchard Road, because it has been going through tough times in recent years. I remember the Chair of the Orchard Road Business Association saying, in a *Sunday Times* article, that what really annoys him is when people say things like, 'Orchard Road now sucks, Orchard Road has no hope.' It does not provide any solutions. I know that planners are looking at Japan's Shibuya crossing, Times Square and Seoul — somehow, despite being expensive cities, they are very liveable. Can you enlighten us on what plans there are for Orchard Road and how they are any different from just building another mall, like what has been done recently?

CKH: I get the sense that you think I can make all these pronouncements on behalf of everybody. To be fair to my colleagues who are in the room, some of whom are from URA, whatever I say does not mean that they are saying it.

Decking over highways and transport infrastructure is a possibility, but the big challenge is the economics. Yes, the airspace is free, but the structure is not, and you have to maintain it. If we ever do it, we would have to be quite selective where we do it, and we have to work out an economic argument. For example, if I were to build a deck and place a park there, I can then release parkland elsewhere for other uses. That is an economic argument. But I would be very careful where I put the deck. I am not too sure that I would want to deck over Orchard Road or Little India. These are huge structures. You have to be very sensitive about it. I can think of some appropriate places where we could do this, but we would have to make an economic argument.

Now, Orchard Road. I am not the expert on Orchard Road. I actually still like Orchard Road! I still go there and I am sure many of you do too. It is not as dire as the way people paint it. The point is that technology and online shopping have affected retail in general.

CHC: It is the death of retail.

CKH: I would not say it is the death of retail. People are very resilient. But for now, the future of retail is a big question mark for many retailers, and there is no real answer. I attend a lot of conferences where they talk about this issue, and people are trying all sorts of things. Some people try the experiential route: you go to a coffee place and you are not just buying coffee, but you do many other things. People are trying all sorts of ways, and we do not know when it will settle down. Even I am trying, because I build neighbourhood centres.

Participant: My question is on the limits of planning. You gave a lot of principles for planning, but I am wondering if, perhaps, there needs to be space for urban experiments; for the community and the citizenry to take up initiatives on their own, for the government to support these initiatives to try out new things, and to respond to changing desires and needs.

CKH: On carrying out urban experiments, consultation, and giving people a lot of free play, we have to understand the context. There are certain things that need to be planned, like infrastructure — power plants, incineration plants, and railway lines. Of course there is still consultation on those, but these really need to be centrally planned. There is less room for experimentation there.

But, as you cascade down to local-level planning, you can actually do a lot of experimentation and co-create spaces with people. I am going to touch a lot on this in the third lecture, and show you examples of how we have worked with our residents, who have offered many wonderful ideas to create the kind of environment that they want. So, yes, you can experiment, but you have to distinguish between different levels of planning and different levels of complexity in consultation and participation.

CHC: I am going to read a question from the audience in the other room. Recently, there was news of how smart lamp posts can, among many things, perform facial recognition. How do you balance the potential of such smart infrastructure to harness this data, with privacy and the rights of citizens?

The second question is: Where do you see the role of the arts and culture, and creativity, in building Singapore 20 years ahead, and how can you enable this?

This third question — you may want to answer it in the next round, it is quite a political question — it is about leasehold. It says: 'Dr Cheong, you mentioned leasehold as a key enabler of land rejuvenation, and I agree with that. But it has also caused anxiety among Singaporeans, especially those living in old HDB flats, with just 40 to 50 years of lease left. People are worried about the value of their assets. Would you convince them that this is still the right model of development?'

CKH: All right, let me start with the smart lamp posts. I suppose the point is not about the lamp post, but about privacy. Yes, this conversation is being held throughout the world. With technology, you need data. Look at Facebook. It is two sides of the same coin. The question is about how to strike a balance. The data is very useful to make living convenient, comfortable, and safe for people. If the police can get the data, it keeps you safe. On the other hand, there is a certain degree of concern about privacy — people might have to give up some privacy.

This is a conversation that will have to take place as we progress towards becoming a Smart Nation. Does maintaining privacy mean that we do not harness technology? No, I do not think so. How you draw that right balance will be a conversation that is very much needed. For some of the agencies that are working on these, they are very mindful of these concerns, and we are just as mindful about protecting the privacy of people. Very often, it is not black or white, because data can be anonymised. For example, we might want to know how many people are on the buses, so that LTA can send out more buses when they know that a particular bus is full. But how do they know it is full? They only know because you tap your fare card and you give the information. My question to you is: Do you want the bus to be full, or not so full? You have to let LTA have the data so that they can put out more buses for you. So, we need to consider both sides. If you want the convenience, you need to allow them to have that data. But that data is anonymised.

For the smart lampposts, I do not know the details of what is going to be fitted there. Counting cars and the number of pedestrians walking and crossing the road is not sensitive. I think you are probably referring to the newspaper report about facial recognition. I cannot really answer on behalf of the police, but when we watch the movies and you want to catch a crook, what do the police do? They have all these cameras in the city, like those in New York, and you look for the crook! So it is not just Singapore. It is everywhere. But it keeps the city safe. These are the issues that we, as a nation and as a society, will have to debate, and make decisions on.

On arts and culture, I am a strong supporter, particularly during my time in URA. We have come a long way. Earlier on, maybe several decades ago, we did not have such a strong arts and culture scene. But, as a planner, I must say that I worked very hard to protect a lot of the heritage and the arts buildings, and I am so pleased that we have a much richer environment. For example, the National Gallery. It is beautiful. I was working to try and repurpose that building, and to renovate it into a beautiful gallery. In fact, I was on the jury panel. So I must say, it has brought a totally new dimension to our lives. I am also a strong supporter of the Esplanade.

But, of course, arts and culture are not cheap to do; it is always about resources and the amount of money that you can give to it. In the last two decades, we have really moved on this, and I think a lot of us enjoy what is there today. But they need patrons. It does not work if you put a building there, and nobody goes to the museum. It would be pointless, right? It needs patrons and supporters, like all of us.

Okay, the leasehold question. Let me try to put it in context. I wanted everyone to understand Singapore's limitations. My interest as an architect-planner is to bring Singapore into the future, to SG100, SG200. Given that you are a small place, how do you ensure that we have facilities and housing for our children and grandchildren, way into the future? In a way, the leasehold land enables us to recover the land for another generation.

HDB flats are sold on 99-year leases. In fact, for HDB flats, you get the full 99-year lease, unlike private developments. The 99 years are meant for a home, enough for two generations. It is a long time, and for most people, after one generation, they can monetise the home. There are many ways to monetise the HDB flat today. You can sell the larger flat, and buy a smaller flat — I build a lot of smaller flats, which a lot of my elderly love, because they really do not want to maintain a big home. With the money, they can put it back into their Central Provident Fund (CPF) and buy CPF Life. If they do want to stay in their own home, they can opt for the lease buyback scheme, whereby HDB buys back some of the lease, and we make sure that you keep the lease that will last you for your lifetime. Another way to monetise is to rent out rooms in their home. There are also people who sell off their flat, to go and live with their children. But if they do not want to stay with their children, they can buy a smaller flat from me. So there are many ways of monetising your flat within the 99 years.

You must remember that, actually, their children will go on to buy an affordable flat from me. Now, how do you make sure that they can buy an affordable flat from me? Eventually, you have to recycle the land. I am trying to paint the broader picture, and there are actually quite a lot of ways to continue to monetise. 99 years is a long time.

CHC: Can I just ask one question, Koon Hean? How many homeowners live in the same flat throughout their lives? Because, surely they would have sold it to somebody else, made some money, bought another apartment, the next person when they buy it at a much shorter lease, will pay much less money. So it is not like they lose the money. Or do they still pay a lot of money for the apartment?

CKH: It is a mix. There are quite a number who still live in their own flats; there are also a lot who monetise. Actually, Singaporeans move house a lot, compared to people in overseas cities. I do not have the statistics here, but I think a lot of people do sell and then move on to something else. So the point really is about making prudent choices. The price you pay for your flat should be commensurate with the lease, and you should buy a flat that will last you your lifetime. These are prudent choices that you should be making.

Participant: My question is about the liveability and lovability of a city. I think Singapore is greatly liveable and very functional. Everything is in order and things work. But, for a city, it is a balance between loveable and liveable, and of course, it is hard to have a city that is both. In your view, how is Singapore doing? Are we going to achieve lovability for Singapore in addition to liveability?

CKH: I think we should try and achieve both. You can be a liveable city. Liveable cities are sometimes easier to achieve because they are things that are built, and you can design it. Lovable is a lot harder to achieve because it involves everybody.

I give these lectures because I wanted to create a greater awareness of what it takes to build and develop a city in this place that we call home, that we love, and to encourage people to love the city, to take part and take ownership. To me, that is what a lovable city is about.

Lovability has a lot more to do with getting people involved, because when people are involved, it makes a world of difference. A city is not so lovable if you just sit there and wait for everybody to do something for you. It is lovable if you are part of the process, and you give back. There is a beauty in giving back. Maybe a lot of you are volunteering or helping others. When you give back, it triggers something in you, a certain emotion, and lovable cities are about emotions. It is about the soul of the city. And sometimes, there are cities that are not very liveable, but people still love the city.

As planners, we try very hard to get people to participate, but you need two hands to clap. Of course planners want to gather feedback, have a conversation, and meet people to try to co-create things. When I talk about HDB, it is a little easier, because you will see more of the real examples. But many of the agencies have, over maybe the last two decades, been trying very hard to do better engagement.

When I talk to my colleagues, I always say it is about touching the emotion. I build public housing. I try and cater to people, and I try to take care of them as well as I can. There must be purpose and meaning behind the job. If a person is not happy about something, there are usually other issues. So you try to look beyond that and say, how can I help you? We cannot always say 'yes', but it is an attitude. Similarly, I feel that engagement is an attitude of saying, can you work with me to do something? In the first lecture, I talked about the weak point we have, which is that we are not very good at persuading. Engagement is not only about people telling us what they want, it is a two-way conversation. It is also about persuading them, on why certain things might need to be done in a certain way.

CHC: Koon Hean, if you would allow me to join in the conversation, because I worked on a topic, 'Asia's Future Cities: Sustainable, Liveable, Lovable'. I played around with the concept of lovability too. Now, you come at it from the point of view of engagement, and that is truly one way of getting at it. But I looked at lovability as, 'Are there sacred spaces in the city?' Secular sacred spaces — it is not about churches or mosques and so on — but sacred spaces that people love and adopt. If you ask Singaporeans, do you have a sacred space in Singapore? Everyone will tell you: Botanic Gardens. That comes up very easily. Some might say, the old National Library — which was pulled down — 'because I dated my first girlfriend there and I married her' and so on. All sacred spaces everywhere seem to have a quiet air about them.

So, cities must have sacred spaces, but sacred spaces are adopted by people, who embrace the space as a sacred space. Planners produce the parameters and they create the configurations, and the space becomes sacred if it is adopted and loved by people, whether it is a park or building. If citizens feel that there are sacred spaces they can adopt, they will come to love the city. This is my place. This is my city. This is my special haven. So that is another take on lovability.

Participant: Do you feel that the complications of housing Singaporeans have become greater? I feel that, in the early days of the housing board, people would tell you about the quality of the flat. Now, they seem to put a high priority on resale value! So they look at the house not only for its living quality, but for what they can make out of it potentially. Does that make the problem of housing Singaporeans a lot more complicated?

CKH: Absolutely! Well, we do remind people often that, first of all, public housing is a home. In the Singapore Conversation a couple of years ago, when we asked people, 'How do you view your public housing? Is it an asset or a home?', it was quite encouraging. Most people came back with the answer that it should be a home first, and an asset second. Therefore, we always say, make prudent choices. Do not speculate on your HDB flat.

Participant: I see a huge pushback on the car-lite initiative; people do not seem to like to take public transport. So what can planners do to get people to change their behaviours, so that we can actually optimise these beautiful plans that you make?

CKH: It is important to give people alternatives if you want them to get off their cars. My colleagues at LTA are trying very hard to build a lot of rail lines. The density of our rail lines will be very high — it will be almost like New York City, and we will be living within ten minutes of a station everywhere. So they are trying very hard, but it takes time. This is the transition period, because you are trying to build, and there is some disruption. But if I am not wrong, more people are taking public transport as more lines open up.

Yes, we need to encourage a switch in people's attitudes towards cars. A dean at the University of Pennsylvania (UPenn) in the US told me that all her students do not drive. They just go for car-sharing, and the car-sharing companies are very novel in the way they do it. Here we have BlueSG, it looks a bit boring. At UPenn, the dean told me that her students who are going out in the evening on a date might pick cars with different colours, even polka dots. The car-sharing companies are so novel in the way they encourage you to get off your own car.

So, technology helps. It is about the last mile, and there is a lot of work being done on making the last mile easy for you. That is why they say: use bicycles. Every time I go home, I see people cycling, because they drop off at the MRT stations, take the bicycle, and cycle home. That is the last mile. We are experimenting with many different alternatives. Right now it is probably a little untidy, but I think in five, 10 years' time, this is likely to change.

CHC: On behalf of the audience, I want to thank you, Koon Hean, for this really inspiring introduction into the awesome planning that has been going on in Singapore.

Lecture III

SHAPING THE FUTURE
OF HEARTLAND LIVING

Introduction

Someone once told me that in Singapore 'HDB flats are like the air we breathe'. They are so much a part of our life because more than 80 per cent of our residential population live in them. Even if you do not live in a Housing & Development Board (HDB) flat, you would have used some of the amenities in an HDB town, be it the market or hawker centre, the neighbourhood shop or clinic. The public housing programme implemented by the HDB over the last 58 years has provided affordable housing for the people of Singapore. It has created a comfortable and convenient living environment for its residents.

Changing Needs and Rethinking the HDB Town

Going forward, there will be trends that affect our HDB towns. In my second lecture, I touched on the trends that will affect us at a national level, and how we take them into consideration in our urban planning for the future. These trends will also cascade down to the local town level. So how should we respond in the way we plan and build our towns? In this lecture, I shall focus on how HDB plans, designs, harnesses technology, and reaches out to

Figure 1: Our HDB homes
(Source: Housing & Development Board)

the community to build better homes together. Some of the key trends which require us to rethink the way we plan our towns are as follows.

(a) An Ageing Population

Singaporeans are living longer and having fewer babies. By 2030, the number of Singaporeans aged 65 and above is projected to double to 900,000, making up 25 per cent of the population, from just one in eight today (Population. sg, 2016).

In planning for towns and estates, we must consider demographic changes. We need to meet the continuum of needs of our residents as they age. Our designs should include suitable accommodation for them, complemented by services that take care of their social well-being and healthcare needs so that they can age-in-place. For example, elderly residents seeking independent living may now prefer to buy smaller flats because these are easier to maintain. The flats should be close to neighbourhood amenities and public transport for convenience, and be served by healthcare and elderly

FEWER WORKING-AGE CITIZENS TO EACH CITIZEN AGED 65 AND ABOVE: CITIZEN OLD-AGE SUPPORT RATIO, 1970–2030

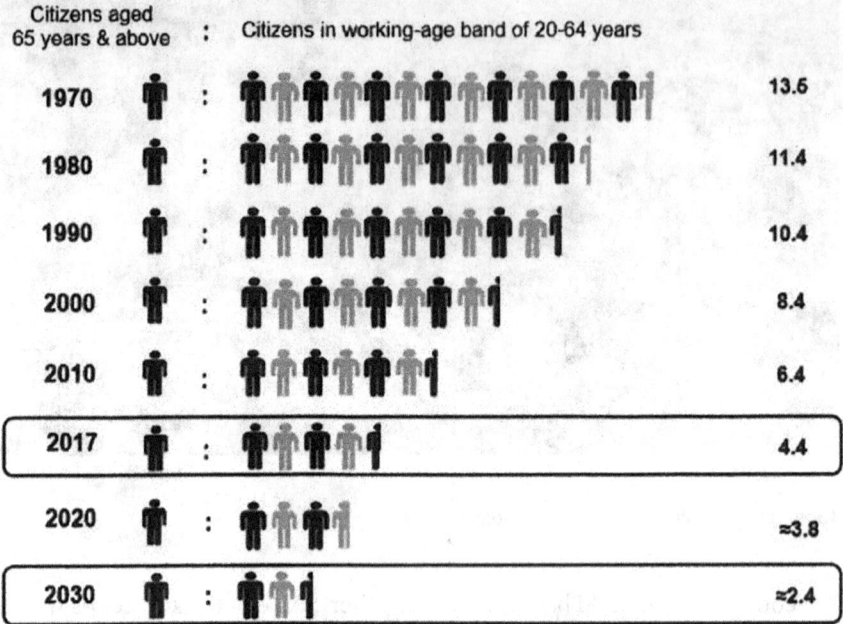

Figure 2: Citizen old-age support ratio from 1970-2030, based on data from Singapore Department of Statistics
(Source: Population in Brief 2017, Strategy Group, Prime Minister's Office, Singapore)

activity centres. Universal design principles should be applied within flats and in public areas, so that mobility is not impeded. We want to encourage and enable the elderly to be physically and mentally active in and outside their homes, so that they are not socially isolated.

(b) Increased Densities

Singapore is a small city-state with a high-density environment. As the population grows, densities may increase further. However, through innovative and thoughtful planning and design, planners and architects can create 'liveable density' by cultivating a pleasant living environment for residents.

(c) Climate Change

Climate change is another phenomenon that we must consider in the formulation of our plans. Increased urbanisation and economic activities globally have led to higher carbon emissions and rising temperatures. Since 1972, Singapore has experienced an increase in warm days and warm nights, and a decrease in cool days and cool nights. On a longer term basis, Singapore's average annual total rainfall since 1980 has increased at an average rate of 100 mm per decade (Meteorological Service Singapore, n.d.). The intensity and frequency of heavy rainfall events are projected to increase as the world gets warmer.

We must, therefore, plan and build in a more sustainable way. In my second lecture, I advocated a circular way of managing our water-energy-food-waste-energy nexus in place of the linear 'use and throw' one, particularly as Singapore is a resource-scarce country. Our buildings should be designed to reduce energy use and encourage natural cooling, so as to reduce the use of air conditioning. Today, HDB already designs for natural ventilation and cooling, and uses renewable energy such as energy generated from solar panels. There are opportunities to use less water and reduce waste, and to re-use and recycle whenever possible. Innovative initiatives, such as the adoption of water-sensitive urban design, could help to mitigate floods.

(d) Ageing Physical Structures and Infrastructure

Recognising that our towns will mature and age over time, HDB began carrying out extensive estate renewal and upgrading of several towns since the 1990s. Where possible, the cycle of improvements and rejuvenation should continue, the pace of which will be subject to the availability of resources. This will ensure that our towns remain a pleasant place to live in, and municipal and estate services are well maintained.

(e) A More Diverse Population

We now have a much more diverse population as we begin to see more inter-ethnic and transnational marriages. More new citizens have also joined us in recent decades (Strategy Group et al., 2017). These trends will increase our diversity in culture, language and lifestyle.

The character of our estates will evolve organically with these changes. We need to find ways to increase community connections so as to promote mutual understanding and social cohesion amongst residents in our towns. The use of design and technology to encourage greater inclusivity and facilitate social interactions becomes even more important. If we do this well, it will help to create a cultural richness and greater community spirit.

At the same time, with increasing wealth and education, people now value their privacy and personal space more. Whilst some may advocate the return of the traditional slab block and common corridor design to encourage more neighbourly encounters, the reality is that the majority of our residents prefer a building layout that gives them privacy. Building the *kampung* spirit will require new design interpretations. Creative designs should strike a balance between building community and making available multiple layers of different spaces — a gradation of public, semi-public and private space.

(f) Rise of Geo-Socialisation and Social Media

I mentioned in Lecture II that the recent trend of 'geo-socialisation' has changed the way people interact. More and more people are now connected through social media regardless of where they live. We can no longer define 'neighbours' by proximity and distance alone. Whilst promoting neighbourly ties by physical design remains important, we need to recognise the presence and power of online communities.

Through technology, virtual communities can cultivate a sense of belonging and civic-mindedness, involving more people to shape and take greater ownership of the environment that they are living in. Netizens with common interests can be brought together to enliven community life. Matching skills to needs, and bringing together residents with common interests across online communities, could be new ways of engendering a *kampung* spirit.

(g) Digital and Technology Changes

Technology and AI will affect almost every aspect of the way we live, work, play and learn.

The future of work

The nature of employment is likely to become more transient with the advent of the gig economy and new freelance jobs. It was reported that, in 2017, there were about 167,000 individuals engaged in freelance work as their primary job (Cheng and Toh, 2017). More people will turn to telecommuting and home offices to perform various jobs from the comfort of their home. These are potential considerations for future flat designs. In fact, some 17,000 HDB flats already operate as home offices today. How can we support citizens in these new roles? For example, we could provide more flexible living spaces that could accommodate suitable types of work that can be done in a home environment, supported by digital infrastructure. As home businesses grow, we could consider providing shared working spaces closer to residential areas or at town centres — which will allow these businesses to expand — and provide telecommunications services and spaces for larger group meetings. These spaces would support entrepreneurship and facilitate start-ups.

The future of retail

Our commercial complexes and shops in the heartlands serve an important social role. They provide convenience and more affordable goods and services for residents. Entrepreneurs just starting out can find more affordable rentals within shops in the heartlands. Many of the shops serve as social nodes, particularly coffee shops where people meet over a cuppa. Residents enjoy familiarity with the shopkeepers, unlike larger shopping malls with chain stores.

At the same time, omni-channel shopping has been growing in popularity. Some have projected that, by 2028, the e-commerce market will grow by more than five times. It would be worth up to $7.5 billion, and make up 6.7 per cent of all retail in Singapore (Tan, 2016). HDB shops need to evolve to cater to the changing shopping preferences of consumers. We could rethink the design of our HDB commercial centres towards a more 'experiential' focus, to attract footfall. In terms of trade mix, more personalised services could be introduced. For example, many Nespresso outlets do not only sell coffee makers and coffee capsules, they offer customers a personalised coffee tasting experience at their coffee bar.

With online shopping, the design of neighbourhoods should be more delivery-friendly. This could mean providing more drop-off and parcel collection points for each block and precinct.

Indeed, the government is looking into an island-wide federated parcel locker network to ease the last-mile delivery challenges. Retailers like NTUC FairPrice are already rolling out Click & Collect lockers that enable customers to collect their groceries after they order them online. The lockers come with refrigerated storage to keep chilled products like milk and cheese cold.

The future of mobility

Autonomous vehicles (AVs) are coming. The push by Land Transport Authority (LTA) towards a car-lite environment and the introduction of autonomous buses require us to rethink the road system in our towns. For example, priority may be given to bus transit corridors while reducing the number of lanes for cars. Many of our multi-storey car parks could be repurposed or redeveloped, should car ownership fall.

A New Generation of Public Housing

HDB ramped up its building programme from 2010 onwards to meet the surge in demand for public housing. Between 2010 and 2017, we launched about 167,000 units of flats. This is equivalent to about five Toa Payoh towns, all launched within the short span of eight years. This is a massive building programme. However, it provided a golden opportunity for HDB to develop a new generation of public housing that would take into consideration the various trends I highlighted above. Rather than just doing more of the same, we wanted to refresh our public housing towns and developments so that they will meet the changing lifestyle needs and rising aspirations of our people. In 2011, we launched the HDB 'Roadmap to Better Living in HDB Towns', which will guide our large development programme over the next few decades. The goal is to build well-designed and community-centric towns that are sustainable and smart.

Thrust One: Well-Designed Towns

HDB does not only build housing. As a master planner and developer, HDB is in the business of developing entire townships. Over the years, the

Figure 3: Three thrusts of HDB's Roadmap to Better Living
(Source: Housing & Development Board)

physical planning of HDB towns has evolved in tandem with the changing socio-economic and demographic conditions of Singapore. However, a few key principles continue to guide the planning and development of our HDB towns. These are:

Planning for self-sufficiency

HDB towns are developed as a total living environment to meet our people's daily needs. Each town should be reasonably self-sufficient. In addition to housing, residents will be well served by shops, schools, social and recreational facilities, etc.

Neighbourhood concept

At the heart of each town is the town centre, which is the key commercial and activity hub. Around it are smaller neighbourhoods of 4,000 to 6,000 flat units, each with its own shops, schools, and parks. Each neighbourhood further comprises precincts of about 400 to 800 units that are also served by a local shop cluster, precinct facilities and green space.

These principles have evolved for newer towns such as Punggol town, where smaller and more intimate and walkable residential estates of 1,200 to 2,800 dwelling units were formed. Each shares a common green space, school and precinct shop cluster.

Checkerboard concept

By juxtaposing low-rise, low-intensity land uses such as parks and schools, with high-rise, high-density residential developments, visual and spatial relief can be achieved to create a pleasant living environment. Community spaces are also better distributed and more accessible to residents.

Hierarchy of facilities

Essentially, larger-scale amenities will serve a wider catchment of residents, while smaller scale amenities cater to localised day-to-day needs. The facilities at different levels comprise:

- Town level: Town plaza, town park, sports complex, integrated transport hub, shopping centres

- Neighbourhood level: Neighbourhood centres, schools, parks

- Precinct level: Precinct pavilion, 3-Generational (3G) play and fitness facilities, community gardens

Planning for connectivity

Our towns are well served by a Mass Rapid Transit (MRT) network, highways and roads. This is now supplemented by more comprehensive cycling and pedestrian networks.

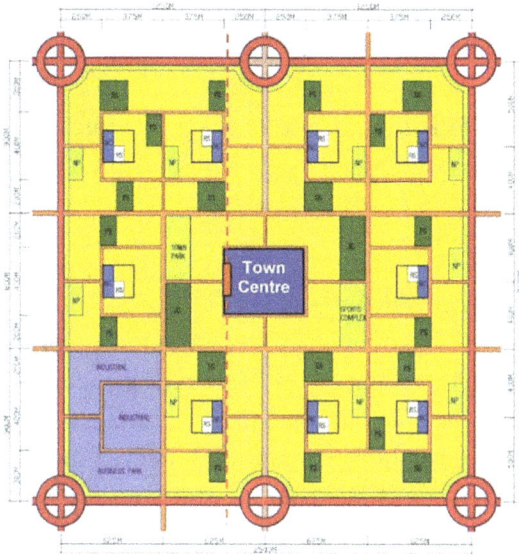

- Juxtaposes high-rise with low-rise developments;

- Neighbourhoods;

- Hierarchy of facilities;

- Well connected and served by public transport

Figure 4: Checkerboard concept of a traditional HDB town structure
(Source: Housing & Development Board)

In addition to the broad principles that have guided the planning of HDB towns to date, we are introducing new strategies to constantly improve the design of our towns. These strategies aim to:

- Develop a new generation of public housing;

- Design an environment that is suitable for all ages; and

- Create synergies from integrated developments.

New generation towns

With the ramp-up of our building programme since 2010, we have had the opportunity to formulate several new master plans for areas such as Punggol North, Bidadari, Tampines North and Tengah. These plans have incorporated fresh ideas, including the following:

(a) More distinctive neighbourhoods and districts

HDB aims to create more distinctive identities for a new generation of towns in greenfield sites, and for areas in the older estates that will undergo redevelopment and rejuvenation. Building 'identity' can help to root residents to home and community. In our planning, we capitalise on 'heritage and place character' to safeguard social memories, and to create a stronger sense of belonging.

(b) Creating green spaces to mitigate high densities

Our homes will be nestled within a garden as we introduce more tropical green and blue water elements in our planning and design. These elements will provide the green lungs and recreational spaces to relieve urban density. More blue elements, such as ponds and streams, will be weaved into the landscape. These elements will be multi-functional, serving to collect storm water, and provide aesthetic and recreational features for our towns.

MORE DISTINCTIVE TOWNS AND DISTRICTS FOR STRONGER IDENTITY

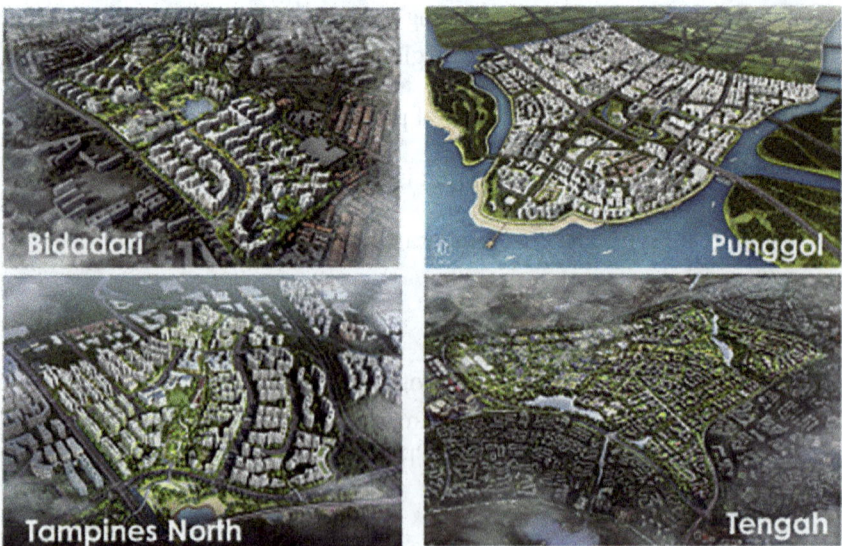

Figure 5: Perspectives showing aerial view of new development areas
(Source: Housing & Development Board)

(c) Focus on quality urban design to sculpt distinctive towns

A key tool to shaping our towns is the use of urban design. In contrast to architecture, which focuses on the design of individual buildings, urban design works to shape a larger group of buildings, streets and public spaces at the whole neighbourhood and district scale, with the goal of making better places for people.

(d) Develop new building typologies and layouts

It is important to carry out quality design at the building and public space levels. We have adopted new building typologies and flat layouts to meet changing lifestyle needs, providing variety and choice, and adding interesting features to the townscape. In addition to the traditional tower and slab blocks, we have introduced typologies such as courtyard housing, terraced housing, housing with decked roof gardens, etc.

Sky gardens and terraces will be selectively introduced to provide residents with a variety of spaces to relax and interact. These sky gardens will create new layers of green spaces to replace ground level green taken up by developments.

Figure 6: Building typologies in 2000s, as seen from (left to right) The Pinnacle@Duxton, SkyTerrace@Dawson and Waterway Terraces
(Source: ARC Studio Architecture + Urbanism, Singapore; Housing & Development Board)

(e) New layouts for new lifestyles

The interior of the flat unit is also undergoing change to meet new lifestyle needs and trends. Kitchen walls have recently been done away with, as many young couples prefer open kitchens. Columns are pushed to the sides

Figure 7: A four-room HDB flat
(Source: Housing & Development Board)

wherever possible, so that residents can have more flexibility in reconfiguring their flat layout. All these improvements enable residents to stamp their own personality on their flat's interior.

(f) A car-lite environment

In line with national efforts, HDB also aims to develop a 'car-lite' environment by encouraging the use of public transport. Almost all our towns are well served by a rail network and well connected bus routes to encourage the use of public transport. Recognising that some may still need to use a car occasionally, LTA has worked with HDB to launch the national Electric Vehicle (EV) Car-Sharing Programme in 2017, where 1,000 cars supplied by BlueSG are being deployed in stages for our residents' use. In addition, the Ministry of Transport (MOT) and LTA are exploring a pilot deployment of AVs as a form of public transport in Punggol and Tengah towns and the Jurong Innovation District, from 2022 (Land Transport Authority, 2017).

To promote the use of alternative modes of transport, comprehensive cycling networks are being weaved into HDB towns to encourage cycling and the use of personal mobility devices (PMDs). The cycling network will also link to parks and park connectors. Towns will be planned to be even more pedestrian-friendly with conveniently connected footpaths, covered linkways, and second storey connections where appropriate, connecting precincts and leading directly to aboveground MRT or Light Rapid Transit stations.

Punggol and Tengah Towns have incorporated many of the new planning and design initiatives (see box stories).

Case One: Punggol Town

Punggol is HDB's first eco-town designed as a 'sustainable waterfront town in the tropics', which will house about 96,000 flat units. The development of Punggol commenced in the 1990s. However, a refreshed vision for Punggol Town's second phase of development was unveiled in 2012, guided by the new key thrusts of HDB's 'Roadmap to Better Living'.

Comprehensive amenities and transportation system

Punggol will continue to be comprehensively planned with amenities, and well served by MRT, with good connectivity via roads and an extensive cycling network. The North East (MRT) line will be extended, with the addition of a station to serve the new Punggol Digital District and the Singapore Institute of Technology.

Signature housing districts

Punggol residents can look forward to seven different waterfront housing districts, namely, Waterway East and Waterway West, Northshore, Matilda, Punggol Point, Crescent and Canal districts. Each district will have its own character, shaped by urban design and new housing typologies.

Integrated green and blue elements will be weaved into Punggol. These include linear green corridors, town parks and waterfront promenades. Punggol Waterway is a man-made waterway that links

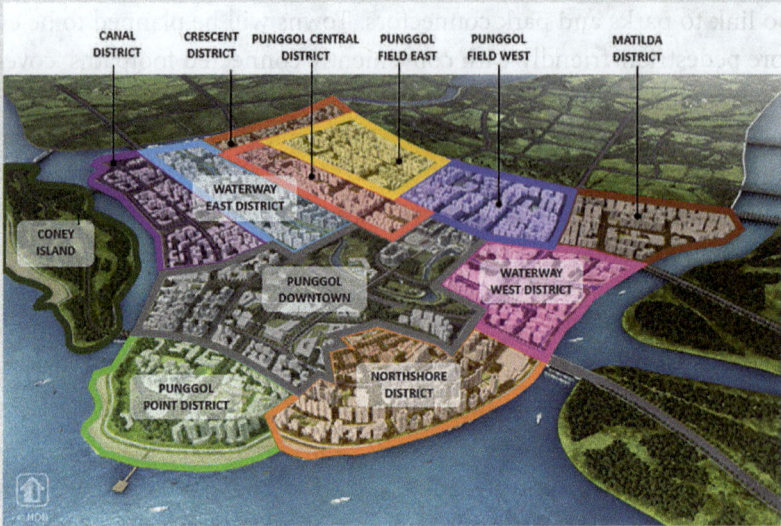

Figure 8: Distinctive districts in Punggol Town
(Source: Housing & Development Board)

two reservoirs, and has since become a signature leisure facility in the town.

My Waterway@Punggol, Punggol Waterway Park, and sports and recreational facilities, such as the SAFRA Punggol clubhouse and the upcoming Punggol Regional Sports Centre, will form the 'Green Heart' of Punggol. Pedestrian and cycling connectivity provided by 'Green Fingers' will also emanate from Punggol's 'Green Heart' towards the coastal promenade and Coney Island. One of the main 'Green Fingers' is Old Punggol Road, which will be pedestrianised and established as a linear landscaped heritage trail, retaining the old connection to the seafront at Punggol Point. This heritage road also runs through the Punggol Digital District and the Singapore Institute of Technology, serving as a linear heritage trail from the heart of town towards the old Punggol waterfront.

Working with other agencies and institutes of higher learning, HDB is developing a Biodiversity Index for its estates. Further research will

Figure 9: My Waterway@Punggol
(Source: Housing & Development Board)

Figure 10: New developments along Punggol Waterway
(Source: Housing & Development Board)

help HDB to draw up a Biophilic Masterplan for Punggol, with a focus on urban greenery, harmonious eco-systems and greater biodiversity.

Urban design guidelines were set out for developments in the various districts. For example, developments along the entire stretch of Punggol Waterway were guided by three different themes (urban, undulating and rustic) with differing built forms (terraced, courtyard and mixed). The end result is the creation of an interesting, changing visual experience as we traverse the waterway.

Case Two: Tengah, An Evergreen Forest Town

HDB's newest town at Tengah falls within a biodiversity corridor between the Western Catchment Area and the Central Catchment Area. Working with the National Parks Board (NParks), HDB formulated a master plan with a 100 metre wide forest belt to safeguard this biodiversity corridor and to connect the green spaces within the town. The Forest theme will be experienced throughout the town. A huge central green lung—the Central Park—will be the green centre of Tengah. Even as Tengah is developed, some of the natural features like its topography and vegetation will be retained. Two storm water collection ponds will be designed to blend in with the landscape as water features and ponds.

Within the neighbourhoods, linear community farmways will be safeguarded for urban farming by the community and perhaps other interested groups, such as social enterprises. These community spaces could encourage residents to bond over shared activities.

A grid road network has been planned to serve Tengah. All the roads that are dual two-lane or wider will have dedicated bus lanes. Transit and mobility corridors will also be safeguarded throughout the town. These corridors include the rail network, bus-priority network and options for possible future forms of mobility such as AVs or PMDs.

Tengah will feature the first car-free town centre in an effort to move towards a car-lite, greener and people-friendly environment.

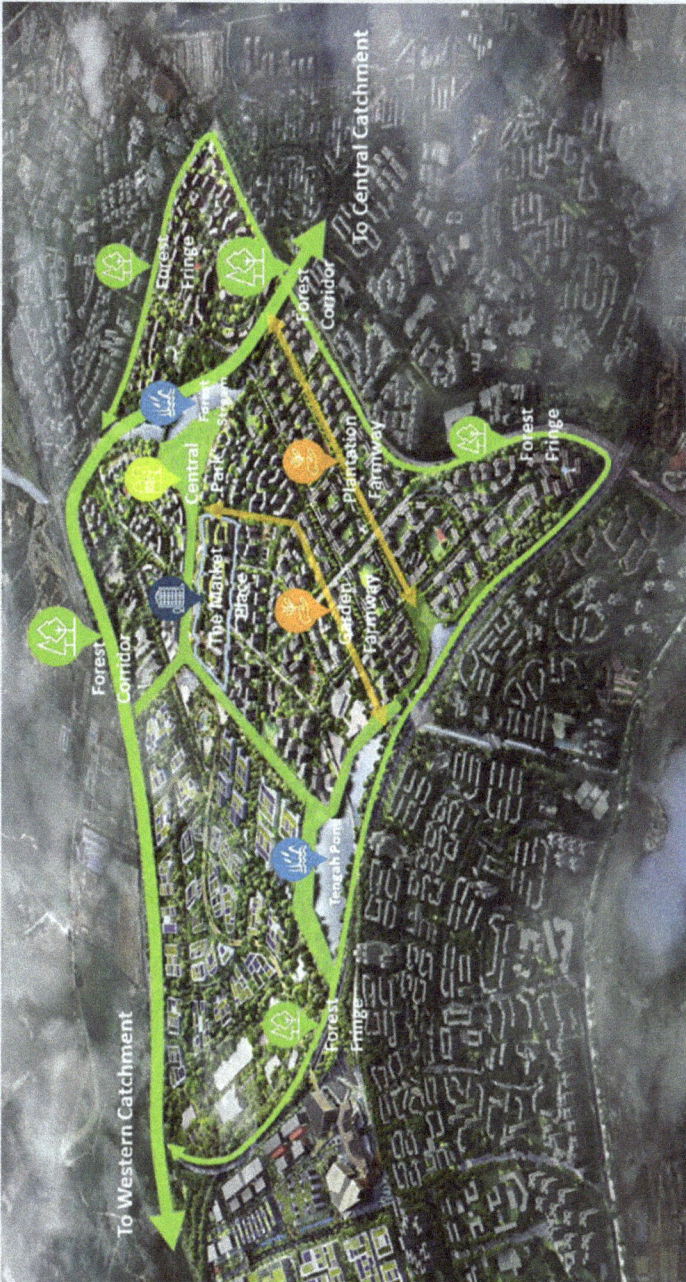

Figure 11: Tengah, the forest town
(Source: Housing & Development Board)

Figure 12: Tengah Town community farmway
(Source: Housing & Development Board)

All roads in Tengah will have dedicated walking and cycling paths on both sides of the road.

Designing an environment for all ages

Today, HDB already adopts universal design principles to ensure that the built environment is usable and accessible to everyone, regardless of age and physical ability. All new flats come with no steps, toilets that can accommodate a wheelchair, and rocker switches that are suitable for the elderly. All existing towns have been retrofitted with ramps to facilitate wheelchair mobility. Through the Lift Upgrading Programme, the majority of flats have access to a lift on every floor.

HDB has actively looked into special housing typologies that are more tailored to elderly needs. Today, a range of housing choices is available for our elderly. For the elderly who would like to live with their families for mutual care and support, we have introduced the three-generation flat, which has four bedrooms, two of which have en-suite bathrooms, so that more people can be accommodated.

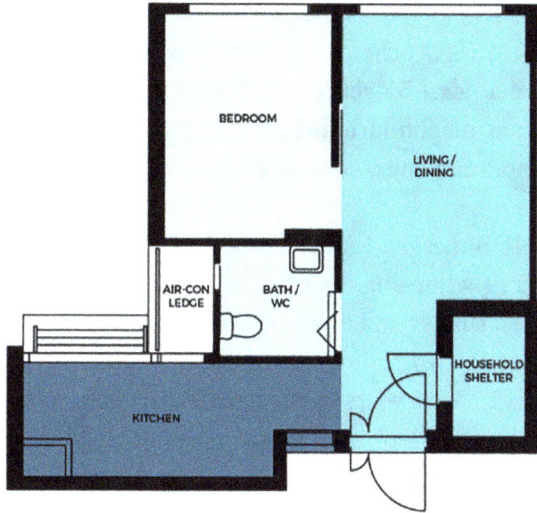

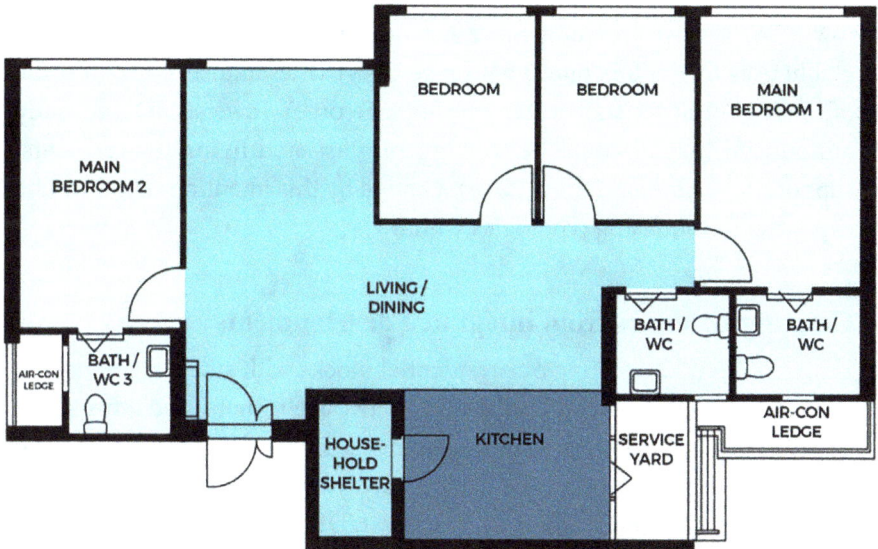

Figure 13: Two-room Flexi flat (top) and 3Gen flat (bottom) floor plans
(Source: Housing & Development Board)

For seniors who prefer to live independently, HDB implemented the Studio Apartment (SA) Scheme in 1998 to offer customised housing for seniors who are at least 55 years old. The SAs are generally located near amenities, such as neighbourhood centres, markets and transport nodes, so that our seniors can enjoy easy access to services, and stay active in the community.

In 2015, HDB merged SAs and two-room flats under the two-room Flexi Scheme, a new housing option to better cater to the diverse housing needs of families, singles and elderly. For seniors, this new scheme allows them to purchase a two-room Flexi flat with flexibility in the choice of lease of between 15 to 45 years in five-year increments, based on their age, needs and preferences. Two-room Flexi flats are available in two sizes — 36 square metres and 45 square metres, and are fitted upfront with grab bars and optional items such as built-in kitchen cabinets and wardrobe.

HDB works closely with the Ministry of Health (MOH) to integrate social and community facilities, including senior care centres, within HDB towns. We are also providing more 'Active Ageing Hubs', which are one-stop clubhouses for seniors offering a range of activities and services, in some of the new projects, such as the one at St. George's Towers. MOH recently announced that it would be looking into assisted living for residents, supported by homecare (Sin, 2018). Guided by this intention, HDB will be exploring new housing typologies with MOH.

Creating synergies from integrated developments

HDB has been co-locating our residential blocks with smaller, compatible facilities such as shops, childcare centres, active ageing hubs, and other social services. However, as integrated developments can yield greater convenience and potential synergies between mixed uses, HDB will consider building larger integrated developments. Recently, HDB led the development of a large integrated development named Kampung Admiralty, which brings together senior housing with commercial facilities, medical and childcare centres, and an Active Ageing Hub (see box story on page 122).

Going forward, there will be more opportunities to carry out integrated developments, particularly in the HDB neighbourhood centres. In 2013,

HDB resumed the development of six neighbourhood centres to better serve residents. These are Oasis Terraces, Buangkok Square, Canberra Plaza, Northshore Plaza, Hougang RiverCourt, and Anchorvale Village.

More will be developed in some of the newer areas in Tengah and Tampines North. We are taking this opportunity to introduce a new generation of neighbourhood centres characterised by the following principles:

(a) Co-locating multiple facilities

Where feasible, HDB will integrate clusters of shops with other facilities such as medical facilities (such as polyclinics), childcare centres, community centres and elderly care facilities. Not only will these developments provide more varied uses for convenience, they optimise the use of land. There are also opportunities to carry out cross-programming among the different facilities. At Kampung Admiralty, popular health talks, cookout sessions, and exercise programmes are held at the Community Plaza. Residents are served by a medical centre, and the hawker centre offers healthy food choices.

(b) Provide public spaces

Public spaces will be provided within the integrated development, to provide convenient and well-designed spaces for the community to carry out their activities and to hang out with family and friends.

(c) Community-centric design

Greater focus will be placed on community-centric design to create more unique developments.

(d) Inputs on tenant mix

Inputs can be sought from residents regarding the tenant mix in the area.

A neighbourhood centre that has just been completed is Oasis Terraces, next to the Punggol Waterway. Facilities such as shops and Food and Beverage (F&B) outlets are co-located with a polyclinic. A unique feature is the roof garden, which looks out to Punggol Waterway. A well-designed, Civic Plaza with a high ceiling will be an attractive public space for holding community activities. The food court and restaurants can be encouraged to tie up with the rooftop community farmers, to cook and sell the community farmers'

Figure 14: Oasis Terraces, new-generation neighbourhood centre
(Source: Housing & Development Board)

produce, and to hold cross-programming events such as farmers' markets. With the Punggol Polyclinic, health and wellness events such as Health Fairs, and Zumba® and yoga practice sessions, can be organised at the large community plaza.

Kampung Admiralty Integrated Development

Kampung Admiralty is conceived as a 'modern kampung' that integrates residential, social, healthcare, communal, commercial and retail facilities all under one roof.

These facilities include:

- Two blocks of housing offering about 100 studio apartments, fitted with elderly-friendly features to facilitate independent and active living for seniors aged 55 years and above.
- The two-storey Admiralty Medical Centre (8,500 square metres), which is a one-stop diagnostic and treatment centre that brings specialist care closer to the community.
- The Active Ageing Hub (about 1,350 square metres) that provides active ageing programmes, such as preventive health and senior learning opportunities, along with centre-based and home care services for frail seniors.
- A childcare centre (about 1,000 square metres) with an estimated 200 childcare places.

Figure 15: Kampung Admiralty Integrated Development
(Source: Lim Weixiang)

Figure 16: Integrated facilities at Kampung Admiralty
(Source: Housing & Development Board)

- Dining and shopping facilities such as a hawker centre offering healthy dining options, and 18 shops and F&B outlets, including a bank and a supermarket.
- A fully sheltered community plaza that serves as a gathering point for residents.
- A community park and community garden that also serve as a roof garden to create new leisure space. It is designed for residents to exercise and to encourage neighbourly interactions through community gardening.

The entire design facilitates interaction between residents of different age groups. Organised programmes, including a range of community health and education programmes by Yishun Health Campus, encourage residents to stay healthy.

Thrust Two: Community-Centric Towns

Beyond being just a provider of homes, HDB also builds active and cohesive communities based on the three pillars of 'software, hardware and heartware'.

Software

To foster social cohesion, the Ethnic Integration Policy (EIP) has been a key policy measure to ensure a good ethnic mix in HDB estates for racial integration and harmony. In recent years, we have introduced the Singapore Permanent Resident (SPR) Quota, which is layered on the EIP to facilitate integration of SPR households in public housing estates.

Hardware

With the community in mind, HDB plans and designs shared spaces and facilities, such as civic plazas, void decks, community living rooms, common green spaces and even 3G playgrounds, to encourage the mixing of different age groups. In addition, we have different flat types for each precinct and block to encourage a more socially inclusive environment.

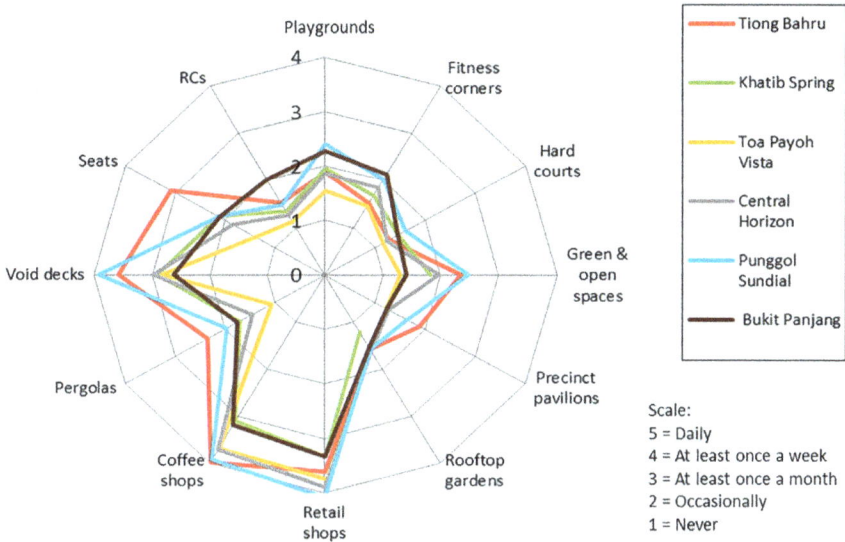

Figure 17: Where residents interact in HDB estates
(Source: Housing & Development Board)

HDB estates host a wealth of spaces where residents get to meet their neighbours incidentally (i.e., unplanned) and convivially (i.e., planned). In an HDB-NUS study in 2014 (Cho and Kong, 2014), it was found that HDB lift lobbies and void decks were conducive spaces for interaction, as well as coffee shops and retail shops. There was positive correlation between amenity usage, and a sense of attachment and belonging. Therefore, well-planned and designed spaces and amenities are critical.

In the design of its new generation towns, HDB has increased the provision of more social and communal places to encourage interaction. These include large town plazas for larger group activities, skyrise greenery,[1] and community living rooms for smaller groups of residents.

Playgrounds are also important social spaces in HDB estates. They play a significant role in bringing families and the community together. From

---

[1] Skyrise greenery refers to rooftop greenery, such as roof gardens and 'green roofs', or the inclusion of plants on vertical surfaces of buildings. For more details, please refer to https://www.nparks.gov.sg/ skyrisegreenery/explore.

the mid-1970s to early 1980s, playgrounds took on distinctive forms, such as dragons and fruits.

Playgrounds built in the early 1990s feature more proprietary play equipment. Three-generation playgrounds were introduced to bring together the young who play there, and older folk who exercise while looking after their children or grandchildren.

HDB has embarked on a new generation of thematic playgrounds in new housing estates. We believe that this will strengthen the town identity and enhance the play experience. For example, Keat Hong estate has a military-themed playground cluster, marking the area's history as a former military camp. As playgrounds are popular gathering points, they can help neighbours and families to develop closer bonds.

Figure 18: The thematic playgrounds at Keat Hong pay homage to the town's military heritage
(Source: Housing & Development Board)

Heartware

The Heartware, comprising people and community, is what makes a town endearing to its residents. In the past five years, HDB has stepped up community-building efforts, by organising activities such as Welcome Parties and HDB's Good Neighbours Awards (Cho and Kong, 2014).

Citizen Engagement

HDB's Sample Household Survey 2013 found that 98 per cent of residents felt a sense of belonging to their town. More than 85 per cent interacted with neighbours of other ethnic groups and nationalities. There was also increasing participation in community activities.

HDB continues to build on these positive trends by encouraging more citizen participation through our various programmes. We would like our residents to play an active role in shaping their environment, take greater ownership in caring for their town, and contribute to building up their community.

HDB works to nurture change makers. They help to promote the spirit of neighbourliness and eco-friendly living in HDB estates. For example, we have 'ambassadors', comprising students and retirees, who volunteer and help spread the eco-living message to residents. Some of our volunteers also initiate activities that add liveliness to places like civic plazas, and foster care and neighbourly relations through organised activities. Other volunteers facilitate community conversations to build consensus on local development and rejuvenation plans. For example, our resident volunteers and student facilitators from tertiary institutions help to lead focus group sessions on how to improve their living environment with our residents.

Figure 19: Co-creating the Tampines Social Linkway
(Source: Housing & Development Board)

Residents are often invited to help co-create places in their estates. One interesting project was the development of a 'Social Linkway' along a pedestrian corridor at Tampines, which was very well used by residents as it leads to their neighbourhood centre. Pop-up stations were set up along the corridor to gather ideas and inputs from residents as they made their way to the neighbourhood centre. Not only did the residents contribute ideas, they also helped to implement several interesting activity nodes, such as a neighbourhood incubator and others for play and learning. There was also an art link with artwork and murals contributed by the residents themselves.

To support ground-up ideas, HDB introduced the 'Friendly Faces, Lively Places Fund' in 2017. Residents are encouraged to draw on this fund to organise events together with their neighbours and the community. Last year, we launched the 'Build a Playground' project to involve the residents and their families in designing and building a playground in their estate. As very positive feedback was received from the first successful playground project built by the community at Canberra, more of such projects will be launched as part of HDB's 'Remaking Our Heartland' programme. HDB has also started to deploy virtual reality (VR) to help residents better visualise the community spaces that they are designing.

HDB also makes it a point to consult the public on its plans. Numerous focus group discussions and exhibitions are held to gather ideas and suggestions for many of our plans before they are formulated or finalised.

Thrust Three: Sustainable and Smart Towns

As the largest housing developer in Singapore, HDB plays its part as a responsible developer to build sustainable towns.

Greater sustainability

In 2011, HDB drew up a holistic and comprehensive Sustainable Development Framework to steer the development of HDB towns.

This framework sets out 10 key desired sustainability outcomes with clear strategies and key performance indicators, which are fully aligned with the national Sustainable Singapore Blueprint. Social sustainability aims to encourage greater inclusiveness and social integration. Economic sustainability strategies focus on creating economic vibrancy and business

PROMOTING SUSTAINABILITY

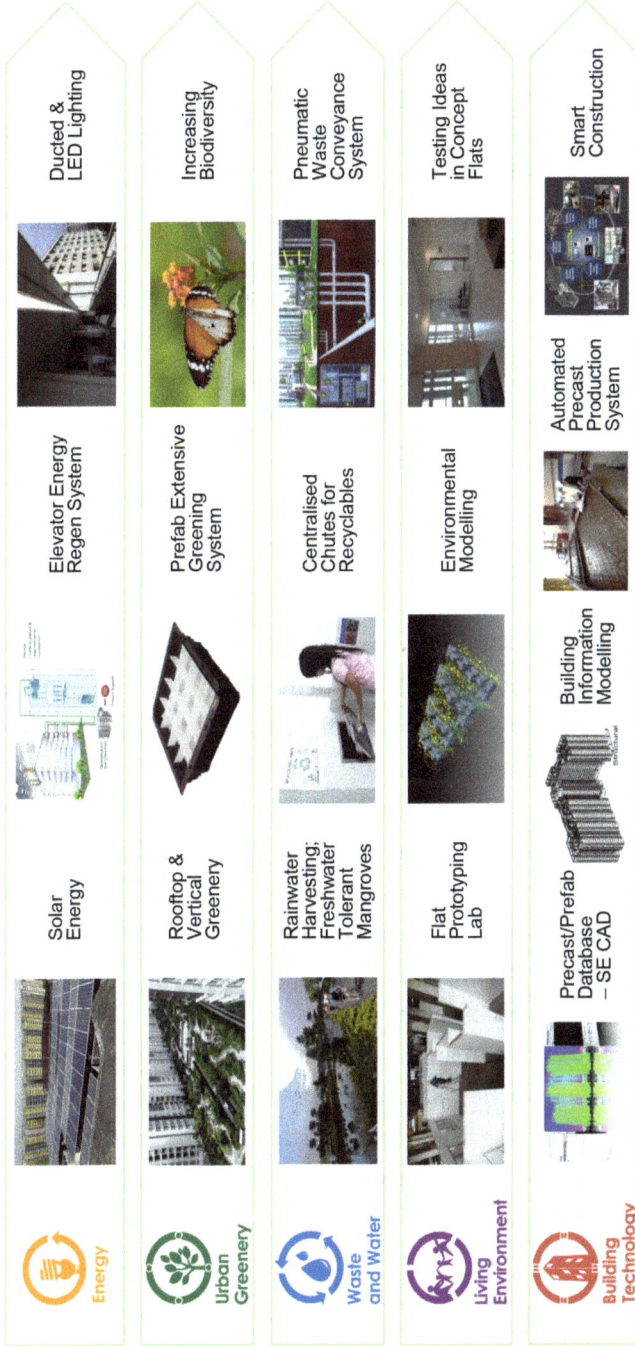

Energy
- Solar Energy
- Elevator Energy Regen System
- Ducted & LED Lighting

Urban Greenery
- Rooftop & Vertical Greenery
- Prefab Extensive Greening System
- Increasing Biodiversity

Waste and Water
- Rainwater Harvesting; Freshwater Tolerant Mangroves
- Centralised Chutes for Recyclables
- Pneumatic Waste Conveyance System

Living Environment
- Flat Prototyping Lab
- Environmental Modelling
- Testing Ideas in Concept Flats

Building Technology
- Precast/Prefab Database – SE CAD
- Building Information Modelling
- Automated Precast Production System
- Smart Construction

Figure 20: Sustainability initiatives
(Source: Housing & Development Board)

diversity, through the provision of innovative commercial facilities within the towns. Environmental sustainability strategies are wide-ranging and include reducing carbon emissions, optimising the use of resources and achieving effective energy, water and waste management. These will provide a clean, safe, healthy and comfortable living environment for our residents. Research is being carried out by HDB in multiple areas on sustainability initiatives.

Various sustainability initiatives have already been adopted by Punggol town. These include extensive greenery to reduce heat build-up; light-emitting diode (LED) lighting and elevator energy regenerative system in lifts to save energy; solar panels to generate renewable energy; centralised chutes for recyclables to increase recycling rates; and rainwater harvesting and water sensitive urban design features to manage storm water. Many of these initiatives were successfully tested in Punggol town and are now being rolled out to other areas and projects.

Enhancing resilience

Mean sea level rise, particularly where it coincides with high tides, presents a risk of coastal inundation of buildings, infrastructure and assets. Various coastal adaptation measures are already being studied by multiple agencies, such as permanent and demountable floodwalls, earth bunds, and floodgates with pumping stations. Not many people are aware that HDB is one of the largest reclamation agencies in Singapore, having reclaimed much of the land in Singapore. Moving forward, HDB will raise the minimum platform levels of reclaimed land to the prevailing codes of the Public Utilities Board (PUB) in anticipation of future sea-level rises.

To cater to a rise in annual total rainfall, HDB has updated its design requirements, and reviewed its drainage requirements for all new projects. HDB is also developing a deeper understanding of climate change issues. For example, it is carrying out research on the use of Urban Water Modelling to simulate water flow and flooding in typical and extreme rainfall conditions, so that we can optimise our water sensitive urban design, and detention and retention features to mitigate flood risks.

The smart HDB town

In line with Singapore's aspirations to become a Smart Nation, HDB will tap on significant innovations in Information and Communications Technology (ICT) to develop smarter HDB towns — making them more liveable, efficient, sustainable and safe. HDB plays a key role in developing smart applications nationally under the Home and Environment domain. To guide the deployment of smart initiatives, we established the **Smart HDB Town Framework**, which comprises two layers:

- **Enabling infrastructure** — This includes the sensing layer (cameras, sensors, Internet of Things, etc.), connectivity and transmission of data, and collection of data to enable big data analytics; and

- **Applications and services** — This includes the applications introduced to serve residents better, and improve the planning, operations and maintenance of HDB towns. These services are grouped under five key dimensions as explained below.

(a) Smart planning

Increasingly, HDB is using sophisticated state-of-the-art computer simulations and data analytics to improve the way we design and plan our towns, precincts and buildings. Collaborating with other agencies such as the National Research Foundation, Singapore Land Authority and the Urban Redevelopment Authority, a three-dimensional city model called Virtual Singapore has been developed, which enables HDB to carry out applications like environmental modelling. Using various computer models, the effects of sun, wind and noise can be simulated so that we can improve our plans before actual development. For example, we could improve the placement and orientation of buildings to channel wind flow through the town, to

DEVELOP A TOWN-WIDE INFRASTRUCTURE

Figure 21: Smart HDB Town Framework
(Source: Housing & Development Board)

SMART PLANNING

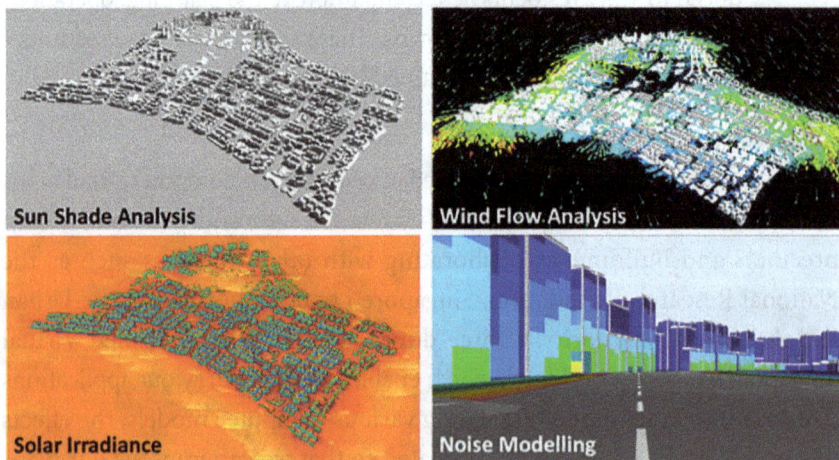

Figure 22: Urban Environmental Modelling
(Source: Housing & Development Board)

create a cooling effect and improve air quality. More greenery could also be introduced at hot spots to reduce heat build-up.[2]

(b) Smart environment

HDB is leveraging sensors to capture real time information about the environment, such as temperature and humidity. Environmental data collected can be used to validate environmental models and carry out proactive upgrading of infrastructure in response to changing weather conditions, in order to create a more pleasant environment for residents.

(c) Smart estate

Using ICT, we can monitor various estate services such as lighting, pumps, solar panels and lifts to better manage the services within the town. HDB has developed Smart Hub, which will serve as a central repository of information received from these sensors. Data analytics can then be carried out to improve the performance and reliability of these services. With AI, predictive studies can also be done. Such data analytics could facilitate proactive detection and intervention to minimise disruption to services.

HDB is looking into the use of drone technology for facade inspections to facilitate timely repairs by the Town Councils.

(d) Smart living

HDB is building 'smart-enabled' homes in our test beds so that residents can benefit from the various smart home applications provided by companies. Such applications include the Elderly Monitoring and Utility Management Systems.

---

[2] Examples of modelling tools include the Planning, Analysis and Exploration Tool, HDB's map-centric application which integrates geo-spatial and textual data for town planning and analysis. The Integrated Environmental Modeller can simulate the combined effects of wind flow, temperature fluctuations and solar irradiance on each other, as well as on the surrounding urban landscape. HDB's City Application Visual Interface can assess the trade-offs among proposed sustainable features in HDB towns and propose the most cost-effective combination of solutions, to achieve the desired sustainability targets.

(e) Smart community

With the collection of data and opinion surveys on demographics, social trends, and lifestyle preferences, HDB will be able to better understand residents' needs and preferences. Suitable applications can be developed to bring communities closer together and empower residents to take greater ownership of their environment, such as in the way common spaces are designed. Data can also be used to nudge residents with gamification tools to help promote eco-living.

HDB is mindful that its research cannot be limited to only technology and engineering solutions. To have a better understanding of societal needs and human behaviour, HDB would have to conduct social and behavioural studies, to better inform its policymaking and spatial solutions. Hence, HDB has recently linked up with the Singapore University of Technology and Design to carry out an extensive research programme called the New Urban Kampung Programme. The findings from this research programme will help to steer HDB in its planning and design of HDB towns.

Using a combination of data from traditional surveys and sensor networks placed around the estate and by engaging the community on and offline, we can better understand our residents' preferences and formulate more targeted improvements in our towns. For example, residents may now place thermal comfort, access to amenities and urban greenery as higher priority. HDB's designs should take these preferences into consideration. Sensors that identify patterns of movement can help HDB to identify under-utilised spaces and finetune the design of these spaces to encourage higher usage. The design of void decks can hence be improved to foster interaction.

Living laboratories

HDB has identified four Living Laboratories to test-bed our various innovations and ideas. These include existing estates at Yuhua and Teck Ghee, and greenfield sites at Punggol and Tengah. Existing estates with residents allow for immediate test-bedding and real time feedback from residents. This enables improvements to urban solutions and applications before these solutions are rolled out on a wider scale to other existing HDB estates and towns in Singapore.

'Age-proofing' older towns

Even as we develop a new generation of public housing, HDB has continued to upgrade our older towns and estates to keep them functional and pleasant to live in. HDB has been 'age-proofing' our towns and flats since the 1990s through multiple upgrading programmes. These programmes focus on both the external areas and interior of flats, and have benefitted thousands of units. These include:

(a) Main Upgrading Programme (or MUP, 1990–2007)

This aimed to upgrade the living environment by providing improvements at the precinct, block and flat levels. The improvements included covered linkways, drop-off porches, fitness corners, residents' corners, toilet upgrading, etc.

(b) Interim Upgrading Programme (or IUP, 1993–2001)

This benefitted flats built between 1981 to 1986 where improvements were made to blocks and precincts.

(c) Lift Upgrading Programme (LUP, introduced in 2001)

It upgraded existing lifts to provide direct lift access on every floor where feasible.

(d) Interim Upgrading Programme Plus (2002–2006)

It combined the IUP and LUP programmes, so that flat owners did not have to wait for the two separate programmes.

(e) Barrier-Free Estate Upgrading (introduced in 2006)

This programme provided barrier-free routes within HDB estates, including the provision of ramps.

(f) Home Improvement Programme (HIP, introduced in 2007)

It focuses on the interior of flats and addresses common maintenance problems in ageing flats, in a systematic and comprehensive manner.

(g) Neighbourhood Renewal Programme (NRP, introduced in 2007)

This programme focuses on precinct and block improvements, such as covered linkways, drop-off porches, playgrounds and fitness corners. It involves the active engagement of residents on the improvements to be provided.

(h) Selective En Bloc Redevelopment (SERS, launched in 1995)
Under this programme, selected old blocks are redeveloped en bloc to optimise land use. Residents in these blocks are given the opportunity to buy new flats at subsidised prices and move to a better living environment served by modern facilities.

(i) Enhancement for Active Seniors (EASE, from 2012)
This programme provides features that enhance the safety and comfort of seniors living in HDB flats to facilitate ageing-in-place. The items include the installation of grab bars, ramps that replace steps, and slip resistant treatment to floor tiles in the toilets. The EASE programme is part of the Home Improvement Programme (HIP), but can also be offered through direct application if there is a need.

(j) HDB Green Print
This is a programme that introduces sustainability initiatives to existing towns. These include initiatives that save energy (using LED lighting, solar panels), save water (using a rainwater harvesting system), and improve waste management (with a pneumatic waste conveyance system). Vertical greenery is also introduced to reduce the urban heat island effect, and cycling paths and bicycle racks are added to encourage greener commute. Yuhua and Teck Ghee were selected as pilot projects.

(k) Revitalisation of Shops (ROS)
HDB works with shop owners and its own tenants to encourage the rejuvenation of retail shops. This is done by co-funding the upgrading of the shopping environment and organising promotional activities, incentivising the renovation of shops and providing a start-up fund for the formation of Merchants' Associations.

(l) Remaking Our Heartland — Blueprint for Renewal
To renew our heartlands in a more comprehensive way, HDB also launched the Remaking Our Heartland (ROH) programme in 2007. Extensive improvements are made to the towns. These could include the redevelopment and upgrading of existing town and neighbourhood centres, injection of new developments, upgrading of parks and playgrounds, introduction of a

cycling network, etc. We have launched three such programmes, benefitting nine towns thus far:

ROH 1 – Dawson, Yishun and Punggol
ROH 2 – Hougang, East Coast and Jurong Lake
ROH 3 – Toa Payoh, Pasir Ris and Woodlands

For ROH 3, the plans were developed from ground-up as planners engaged the public through focus groups, so that our residents could help to co-create the plans.

Conclusion

Our HDB towns will continue to be at the heart of Singapore living. HDB has a huge task — to develop and maintain an environment that will enable our people to live comfortably and build families and friendships. Planners and architects will need to draw on their creativity and resourcefulness to develop liveable environments within available land and resources. HDB will continue to look to technology to set the stage for new urban solutions.

Today, in partnership with communities and residents, HDB is developing many exciting plans for our estates. We know that HDB estates are not only about physical buildings and infrastructure. Our plans are only fully realised when they become homes for our communities and families. Our residents play a very important role as they have a great impact on the living environment too. They greatly influence towns and neighbourhoods through their civic actions and consideration for neighbours, and their sense of ownership by caring for both their home and the surrounding environs. HDB needs a strong partnership with Singaporeans to build a good home together.

References

Cheng K., and Toh, E. M. (2017, May 19). The big read: The unstoppable march of the gig economy. *Today*. Retrieved from https://www.todayonline.com/singapore/big-read-unstoppable-march-gig-economy

Housing & Development Board. (2016). Good Neighbour Award. Retrieved from https://www.hdb.gov.sg/cs/infoweb/community/caring-for-your-neighbours/good-neighbours-movement-page/good-neighbour-award-2017

Housing & Development Board. (2017, May 29). Community: Welcome party. Retrieved from https://www.hdb.gov.sg/cs/infoweb/community/care-for-your-neighbours/get-to-know-your-neighbours/welcome-part

Im, S. C., and Kong, C. H. (2014, May 21). HDB/NUS study on impact of built environment on community bonding. Retrieved from https://www.hdb.gov.sg/cs/infoweb/doc/community-seminar-nus

Land Transport Authority. (2017, November 22). Autonomous vehicles to transform intra-town travel by 2022. Joint news release by the Land Transport Authority and Ministry of Transport. Retrieved from https://www.lta.gov.sg/apps/news/page.aspx?c=2&id=39787c15-ad56-4d1a-8ba9-4ea14860f9b4

Meteorological Service Singapore. (n.d.). Past climate trends. Retrieved from http://www.weather.gov.sg/climate-past-climate-trends/

NParks. (n.d.) Skyrise greenery: Explore. Retrieved from https://www.nparks.gov.sg/skyrisegreenery/explore

Population.sg. (2016, August 22). Older Singaporeans to double by 2030. Retrieved from https://www.population.sg/articles/older-singaporeans-to-double-by-2030

Sin, Y. (2018, January 28). More home-based care options likely for seniors. *The Straits Times.* Retrieved from https://www.straitstimes.com/singapore/housing/more-home-based-care-options-likely-for-seniors

Strategy Group, Prime Minister's Office, Singapore Department of Statistics, Ministry of Home Affairs, Immigration & Checkpoints Authority, and Ministry of Manpower. *Population in Brief 2017.* Retrieved from https://www.strategygroup.gov.sg/docs/default-source/default-document-library/population-in-brief-2017.pdf

Tan, W. (2016, May 24). S'pore e-commerce market will grow to S$7.5b in 10 years. *Today.* Retrieved from https://www.todayonline.com/business/google-temasek-see-s-e-asia-web-economy-reaching-us200-billion

Question-and-Answer Session

Moderated by Professor Lily Kong

Professor Lily Kong (LK): As a professor of geography, I find this talk to be especially interesting because the work of geographers is often about space, and the making of spaces for the betterment of the human condition.

When I studied urban geography and looked into our housing history, I learnt, over the years, to recite this narrative about our housing landscape. In the 1960s and the 1970s, it was about a shortage of housing, and the need to break the backbone of our housing shortage. And that happened. First, SIT — not the Singapore Institute of Technology but the Singapore Improvement Trust — did its part, and it tried, but it did not quite succeed. Then, HDB, when it was set up, managed to break the backbone of the housing shortage in the 1960s, into the 1970s.

But soon after the quantitative targets were reached, there was recognition and a sense that housing is not just a roof over our heads — it is also about identity and character, about social interaction, and that was a time when there were sociologists hired by HDB to help with the research and understand how to encourage greater social interaction. The concept of 'precincts', for example, was developed. I recall my colleague, Chua Beng Huat, talking about how, when he was a sociologist in HDB, he would study the number of households or housing units that would make for optimum interaction.

So, social interaction and the character and identity of estates were given more attention in the 1980s and the 1990s. And of course in the 2000s through to the present, you see a whole host of initiatives, ranging from the use of technology to enhance our lifestyles, to the attention paid to history and heritage, place-making, the sense of community, and so forth. A great deal has been done over the years, and you can trace the development of HDB efforts.

So, my question is, looking ahead, with all the many wonderful things that have been done and continue to be done, are there gaps that you think HDB might want to try and plug in future, from the spatial planning, physical infrastructure perspective. What might those opportunities be?

While I let Koon Hean think a little about it, I would like to give a heads-up to the young people and students in the audience — Koon Hean would particularly like to hear your comments, questions and reactions. For the young at heart, you also have an opportunity to ask questions, but if there are more hands than not, I am going to give the opportunity to the young students, with your indulgence.

And now, back to Koon Hean. Do you have some thoughts about my opening question?

Dr Cheong Koon Hean (CKH): Thank you, Lily. Okay, gaps. We are always trying to improve. Sometimes, when I read comments about HDB's designs, people forget that there are different decades of HDB designs. In the old days, of course, things were quite basic, and cost was a factor. People forget the other side of the formula, that there is a cost to doing things. Over the years, we have gone from very basic to much better designs. And now, there is the introduction of more science and technology. With that, we can improve the designs of the towns. The gaps are at different levels: at the town level, at the precinct level, at the building level. At the town level, it is a little more sophisticated going forward to build sustainable towns, with the help of computers.

In the old days, planning was very intuitive, yet my predecessors were sustainable in their approach. I learnt from my colleagues that they had always planned for natural wind flow. That was before the word 'sustainable' became part of our vocabulary. If you look at many of the towns, they were planned for a good cooling effect.

The other thing that we could work better on is the public spaces, whether they are civic plazas or void decks. I do not like the word 'void decks'. I call them 'community living rooms'. That is a lot friendlier. I think we can improve them. It requires a better understanding of how people use these spaces. That is where science and the New Urban Kampung research study are very important, so that we can design better with deeper insights.

Going forward, there will be changes in behaviour, such as whether people will drive or not, and so the way we plan will also change. It is always a work-in-progress.

I think it is also important to work with residents. When we work with residents, it is not about asking, 'What do you want?' It is easy to ask people what they want; and for them to say these are the 1,000 things they want. Rather, it is an engagement. That is why the virtual reality application I showed earlier is very useful. We can explain that when you design this place, this is your budget. The conversation has to take place within certain parameters to be constructive, and I would like to see residents take greater ownership of their environment.

You can design all these spaces but if people throw rubbish down from the top, what can you do? How can we keep the estate in a pleasant condition? It takes two hands to clap. It is not about 'what can you do for me?' — it is about what can we do together! So, when you ask such a question, I will say to you, 'together'!

LK: I must learn that trick for the classroom!

CKH: Students get special dispensation!

LK: Now, I am going to take a few questions at a time.

Participant: I speak on behalf of the Disabled People's Association (DPA). I think one basic gap at the building level is the fire safety issue. Just a month ago, at Block 8, North Bridge Road, there was a fire, and that highlights the risks that we face when we evacuate people — or 80 per cent of our population, who stay in HDB flats. I understand that there are provisions in high-rise condominiums of above 26 metres to have a fire lift with backup generators, and an empty or refuge space for wheelchair users as a temporary holding area. But such features are missing from HDB flats, where 80 per cent of us live. Is this a gap that can be addressed? Certainly, we want to work together; DPA would certainly like to work with HDB, the Singapore Civil Defence Force (SCDF), as well as the Building & Construction Authority (BCA) on this issue.

Participant: Hi Dr Cheong, I am a property agent. I must say that HDB has improved over the years. But as I was looking at it, there is a divergence in terms of pricing between old and new flats for the older generation and the younger generation, between rich Singaporeans and poor Singaporeans. So to me, when I look at my clients, one is rich, one is poor, one is old and one is youngish and all that, I sense a social divide, rather than a unity. It is a rather pressing social problem for me. Maybe it is a ticking time bomb. Sometimes I feel caught between the two of them. When I survey them, some say, 'Maybe just live in Johor Bahru, because it is cheaper.'

LK: I am sorry to interrupt but in the interest of letting others have a chance, could you summarise your question, please?

Participant: This matter of ownership: Is it real ownership or tenancy? In Singapore, is it a home or hotel, a country or corporation?

Participant: I can see that you are very proud of HDB. So are many Singaporeans, including me. My question is, in the last lecture, you mentioned that Singapore's population density would increase in the future. I can understand and appreciate your views on higher population density based on your role as a planner, not a policy-maker, but planners, too, do not plan in a vacuum. My question is, what underlying principles or philosophies guide your planning processes?

Participant: If distinctiveness is the preservation of heritage and memory, then how do we decide what to preserve, considering that, for example, for the sake of experiential shopping, we sacrifice our HDB *mamak* shops? How do we decide that, for example, Old Punggol Road is worth preserving over some other pieces of our heritage?

Participant: My question is related to your point on 'real people'. You said just now that you are dealing with real people. What I remember from my time dealing with HDB, before I became a Member of Parliament, was about the reality of multi-cultural living. But in your context, given the real people of today and the future, how do you see HDB coping with the new Singapore, the new normal, and the real people in the political contexts?

Participant: This is a more technical question. We use a lot of concrete in our buildings and somehow they trap heat, especially in our tropical climate. I am wondering if HDB is experimenting with bamboo or other materials that can reduce the heat on the surface of our buildings?

LK: Sorry, Koon Hean, there were six individuals and 20 questions.

CKH: Okay, thank you for all your questions.

I would like to answer [the student participant] first. One of the reasons for giving these lectures is because I wanted to talk to the young people. The way I had arranged my lectures is to give a better understanding of what it takes to make this place better. Especially when we are a city-state with constraints that Janadas [Devan] had talked about: land constraints and resource constraints. I am happy that you asked the question.

Distinctiveness — yes, who is the judge? Actually, you are the judge. This is about participatory planning, which I talked about in Lecture I. Seoul was a good example of participatory planning. It is a process, which, I confess, we are still learning. Who decides what is distinctive? There is no homogeneity on this. Let me give one example. When we did our Remaking Our Heartlands (ROH) project, for ROH 1 and ROH 2, planners tended to do the design, and then ask, 'What do you think?' Then you give your feedback, either you like it or you do not like it, and we will change the plan.

Then for ROH 3, we changed the process. We decided that we should not even do the design first. We started by engaging the residents. We had a lot of focus group discussions, and we asked them, 'You have lived in this town, right? What do you remember most about this town? Where do you meet your friends? What do you like about this town, and what don't you like about this town?' From there, we developed the brief for the plan; only then do we try to put things together. But of course, the most difficult part is, one person likes the plan but another does not. Participatory planning is about hearing all views — in the end, you have to make a decision. You cannot satisfy a hundred per cent, but at least through this process, if you cannot give people something, you can explain why. That is the process.

So really, it is not 'who decides' but 'how can we decide together?' That is a very difficult process. This is why there is a lot we can learn from Seoul. They have a lot of different voices and, yet, they were able to do some very difficult projects, such as removing the roads. It is a process that we need.

You asked about *mamak* shops because it is in the news, right? Lifestyles change, and so do the economics which you need to consider. It is the same with conservation, which I talked about in my second lecture. How do you keep some of these traditional trades? I asked how many of you would buy the *cha kiak* [wooden clogs] today? If nobody buys the *cha kiak*, how am I going to keep those shops running? They will not be economically viable.

These are some of the issues that not only Singapore struggles with; it is a struggle all over the world, including Japan, which has a lot of mom-and-pop shops. I take a slightly more pragmatic approach — you give them as much help as you can, but they have to be economic, because otherwise, they will not survive. So I pose the question back to you. How would you do it? Do you give them a lot of subsidies, which is taxpayers' money? Are you going to buy from the guy downstairs? If you do not buy from him, well, I rest my case. So think about that.

There are some very technical questions like the use of bamboo. I am not an engineer, but I have a lot of engineers sitting here — you can ask them later as my colleagues are doing research and development. But I did read about bamboo, and I think it is quite an interesting material. I do not know enough about it, but it is certainly something we can look at. But again, scale is something we need to consider. In HDB, we build on such a huge scale. I do not know if some of these materials can cater to the type of scale that we build to.

Now, on the question about fire safety and the disabled, I think there was a reply on this in the press. We looked through the building codes together with SCDF, and we do comply with the codes. I would be happy to take this offline with you. I believe the SCDF is also talking to you. The code does take your concerns into consideration. We do want to take care of the disabled and from what I recall, the code can cater to them. So feel free to come and talk to us, and the SCDF.

Your question [on real people] is quite a tough one — I thought you should be answering it as the ex-politician! [Laughter]. It is not easy to deal with. You know because you meet residents when you do your walkabouts.

It is not easy for HDB. When you have so many people living together, trying to get people to live together harmoniously is challenging. The tool we have is a spatial one: I build for you spaces, housing, and through some policies, such as the Ethnic Integration Policy (EIP), we mix people, nationalities, different types of flats, but the tools are essentially spatial.

HDB on its own does not have the full set of tools to achieve social cohesion. We are only one part of the solution. There are many parts. It is also about how you convince people to be more accepting of people of a different nationality, to be a little bit forbearing because we all have different cultures and habits. However, even when someone has a problem with their neighbour because there is a little bit of noise, they do not knock on the door of the neighbour and say, 'Excuse me, can you just tone it down?' They call us and say, 'Can you tell him to tone down!' Now, if you have good suggestions, I would be happy to take them on board and learn from all of you, because this is my point about doing it together.

LK: We are running short of time, and I know people are already moving off, but there were two other questions from the spillover room that were handed to me, and I feel that I should give them the time of day. They are both related to technology. One is about new technologies in the form of personal mobility devices, and how HDB towns would cater to them. The second question is related to technology in the home, and something you said about human behaviour. So you have the sensors in the home, but some of our elderly folk put towels over them to cover them, because they do not want people looking at them, or you have a panic button for them but they keep it away somewhere safe, in case they press it accidentally. How do we get around some of these issues, where there is availability of technology, but human behaviour does not necessarily take the form that we assume they will?

CKH: They are very good questions and we struggle with these issues too. Let me give you an example. We tested the elderly monitoring system. You have to try it in a place where there are human beings, so we actually trialled in a lot of flats and we got some of the elderly residents to volunteer. By the way, let me clarify that these are sensors, not cameras, otherwise the residents will feel very shy if you put them near the toilet. The sensors sense movement and do not actually capture you visually. After we put in the sensors, we get them to give us their feedback. 'Do you understand how to use it? Are you disturbed by it?' They were very happy. There was no problem and it was very simple to use. So you must trial with real people. And of course, you need to educate people about technology.

Worldwide, there will be a divide between people who know technology and people who do not, and we talked about this at the last lecture. Therefore, we need to teach people and bridge this divide, otherwise there will be inequity.

Having said this, let me end with a story. I have an aunt and she is almost 75, 76 years old. So when she came — she does not live here, she lives in Malaysia — she was very excited because my son taught her how to use WhatsApp and to go on the Internet. Now she is WhatsApp-ing everybody, reading all the news and watching all the movies on the phone. So there is hope because we can all be taught. This is the point. And we must make the technology disappear, to make it a non-issue for people. And that is the responsibility of all designers, all of us who introduce technology.

LK: I will not attempt to summarise the discussion, because we have covered such a wide spectrum of issues and themes that HDB deals with — from the social, spatial, technological, and historical, to looking forward into the future. I think it is evident to all that HDB has a real challenge on its hands. It is not just about providing roofs over people's heads, but about building community, and understanding human behaviour while trying to figure out how science and technology can be harnessed for the best use, for a better living environment. It is a very multifaceted and complex organisation, which has a whole host of different responsibilities, and I think we owe it to the CEO who is sitting with us, to thank them for all their efforts in trying to house a nation.

So if I might invite you to join me in thanking Koon Hean for a very interesting and enlightening discussion, and more so for the work that HDB and all her colleagues who are seated here do on a daily basis. Thank you.

About the Cover Illustrator

Caleb Tan ("Bucketcaleb") is an illustrator from Singapore. He graduated from the School of Technology for the Arts, Republic Polytechnic in 2009. Caleb illustrated a Singapore children's book with Direct Life Foundation and AF Storytellers, which was launched in 2016. He works closely with the Organisation of Illustrators Council (Singapore).